OWLING

Enter the World of the MYSTERIOUS BIRDS of the NIGHT

MARK WILSON

Storey Publishing

The mission of Storey Publishing is to serve our customers by
publishing practical information that encourages
personal independence in harmony with the environment.

Edited by Deborah Burns and Lisa H. Hiley
Art direction and book design by Jessica Armstrong
Text production by Erin Dawson
Indexed by Nancy D. Wood

Cover photography by © Mark Wilson, except front,
    background, by Free Nature Stock/Pexels
    .com; inside back, author, by © Jean Herrick
Spine graphic by © curly pat/Shutterstock.com
Interior photography by © Mark Wilson
Additional interior photography by © Aaron D. Flesch, 27
    #6, 62 l., 63; © All Canada Photos/Alamy Stock Photo,
    48, 83 l.; © B. E. McGowan Photography/Getty Images,
    51 b.; © Bruno Kern, 29 t., 79 t.r.; © Carrie Wendt, 41
    t., 112 t.r. & m.r.; © curly pat/Shutterstock.com, inside
    cover, background; © Donald M. Jones/Minden Pictures/
    Getty Images, 11 b.l.; © Glenn Bartley/Getty Images, 62
    r.; © Jamie Pringle, 56 b.; © Jessie Roughgarden, 112 l. &
    b.r., 113; Kathy & Sam, Beaverton OR, USA/Wikimedia
    Commons, 32 #4; © Ken Shults, 45 t.l., 60 l., 76 t.l.;
    © Konrad Wothe/Minden Pictures/Getty Images, 26 #4;
    © Rolf Nussbaumer/Getty Images, 40; © Mint Images —
    Frans Lanting/Getty Images, 13 row 3 l.; © Paul Bannick/
    PaulBannick.com, 13 row 5 c., 32 #3, 43 t.r., 45 t.r., 61 t.l
    & b., 64 l., 83 r.; © Rick Evets, 19 b.l., 70 b., 80 l.; © Rob
    Lowry, 43 t.l., 45 b.; © Skip Moody/Dembinsky Photo
    Associates/Alamy Stock Photo, 11 t.; © steve young/Alamy
    Stock Photo, 101 2nd from t.; © Tom Uhiman/Alamy Stock
    Photo, 13 row 4 r.; © Tom Vezo/Minden Pictures, 65 t.
Illustrations by © Jada Fitch
Range maps and silhouettes by Ilona Sherratt. Range
    maps adapted from The Cornell Lab of Ornithology
    All About Birds website, www.allaboutbirds.org.

Text © 2019 by Mark Wilson

Storey books are available at special discounts when
purchased in bulk for premiums and sales promotions as
well as for fund-raising or educational use. Special editions
or book excerpts can also be created to specification. For
details, please call 800-827-8673, or send an email to
sales@storey.com.

Storey Publishing
210 MASS MoCA Way
North Adams, MA 01247
storey.com

PRINTED IN CHINA BY R.R. DONNELLEY
10 9 8 7 6 5 4 3

Library of Congress Cataloging-in-Publication Data

Names: Wilson, Mark Chester, 1959– author.
Title: Owling : enter the world of the mysterious birds of
    the night / Mark Wilson.
Description: North Adams, MA : Storey Publishing,
    [2019] | Audience: Age 8–12. | Audience: Grade 4 to 6.
    | Includes bibliographical references and index.
Identifiers: LCCN 2018041436 (print) | LCCN
    2018043463 (ebook) | ISBN 9781612129631 (ebook)
    | ISBN 9781612129624 (hardcover with glow-in-the-
    dark ink on cover : alk. paper)
Subjects: LCSH: Owls—Juvenile literature.
Classification: LCC QL696.S8 (ebook) | LCC QL696.S8
    W55 2019 (print) | DDC 598.9/7—dc23
LC record available at https://lccn.loc.gov/2018041436

FRONT COVER OWLS, from left to right: Eastern Screech-Owl, red
morph; Snowy Owl; Flammulated Owl; Great Horned Owl; Barn Owl;
Great Gray Owl; Northern Saw-whet Owl

OPPOSITE PAGE OWLS, clockwise: Great Gray Owl; Short-eared
Owl; Great Horned Owl adult and large chick; Snowy Owl

⟫ CONTENTS ⟪

»1« All about OWLS

YOU MIGHT NOT REALIZE IT, BUT YOU NEED TO SEE AN OWL. Not in a zoo or a museum but in the wild, uncaged and free. But how do you even find an owl, never mind spend time watching it?

Maybe you will hear a distant hoot outside your bedroom window or, if you're lucky, glimpse a passing shadow in the night woods. But mostly, owls seem unknowable, even invisible. Sometimes it seems like you'd have more chance of seeing Bigfoot. Or maybe a unicorn. But owls are real and they live around you, maybe closer than you think. You just need to know more about them.

Owls may be living closer to you than you realize. Is there an owl in your backyard?

Let's venture into the secret world of owls, a world most people will never know. Bring your questions, as well as sharp eyes and eager ears. The owls are waiting and watching for your arrival.

RIGHT: A Barred Owl studies a visitor to its woods.
OPPOSITE: A Great Gray Owl sweeps silently across a snowy field, hunting for voles tunneling beneath the white blanket.

Even people who know very little about birds can identify an owl. No one mistakes an owl, with its big head, large eyes, and imposing presence, for any other kind of bird.

Why do owls fascinate us so? Is it because they are **raptors**, flying predators that swoop down on squirrels, grab ducks out of the water, and snatch insects, other birds, and even bats from the evening air? Those sharp **talons** (claws) mounted on powerful feet are most impressive.

Perhaps the magic starts in the owl's face, specifically the eyes. Those huge, impossible-to-ignore eyes, facing forward with an intense expression, immediately capture our attention and affection. With their all-seeing eyes, owls not only look *at* you but seem to look *through* you. It's almost as if they can read your mind!

When you lock eyes with an owl, the stare-down can be a bit unnerving. It's hard to look away, but no one ever wins a staring contest with an owl.

WISE OLD OWL?

An owl may remind you of a person — stern, serious, sometimes cranky, but lovable. Big saucers of fine feathers, called **facial disks**, encircle the eyes of many owl species, framing its stare. The owl's all-knowing air is reinforced by its ability to turn its head more than half-way around in each direction.

Their large eyes give owls an air of intelligence that — let's be honest here — they haven't necessarily earned.

Because their eyes face forward like human eyes, we are tempted to believe that owls think like us. Those huge eyes give the owl its keen sight, but they mean less room in the skull for the brain. Owls aren't like ravens, which can count; or crows, which can fashion tools from twigs; or African grey parrots, which can learn enough words to communicate with people. Owls do have good memories, though.

Owls look smarter than they really are.

Parts of an Owl Head

ear tuft

facial disk

crown

forehead

eyebrow

cere

beak

pupil

iris

Screech-Owl

Burrowing Owl

How come owls have a unibrow?

The facial disks, which come together to form one large over-hanging eyebrow, add to the intense look of the owl. The disks also act like the brim of a baseball cap and help shade the eyes from direct sunlight.

Why do some owls have ear tufts?

Ear tufts might be useful for camouflage, or maybe to help the owls communicate their moods. It's possible that ear tufts catch sound from behind the owl and direct it into the ears. More research on owl ears is needed!

Inside & Out

Even though owls are shaped very differently from humans, many of their bones are similar to ours.

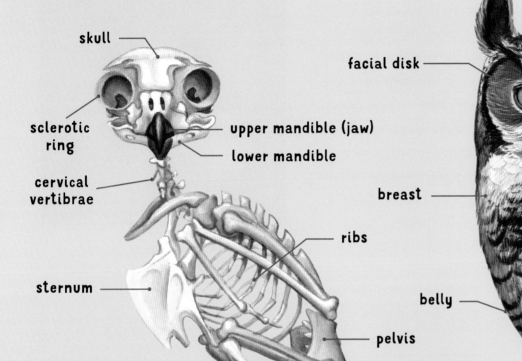

skull

sclerotic ring

cervical vertibrae

sternum

fibula

tarsometatarsus

toes

upper mandible (jaw)

lower mandible

ribs

pelvis

femur

facial disk

breast

belly

tail

How can owls turn their heads so far around?

Owls have 14 vertebrae in their necks. You have 7. More neck bones create more joints, which allow owls to turn their heads farther around than we can. A specialized blood supply to the brain ensures that owls don't pass out when they turn their heads extra far.

What kind of bones do owls have in their wings?

Underneath the feathers, wings are like arms. Some of the bones even have the same names.

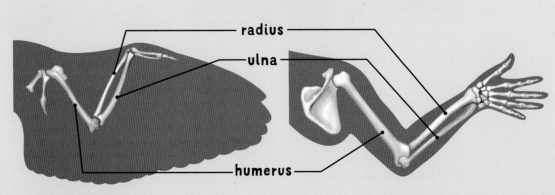

radius

ulna

humerus

OWL

HUMAN

TURNING IN CIRCLES?

People often ask, "Can an owl turn its head in a complete circle?" The answer is yes and no.

A full circle is 360 degrees. Most references confidently state that owls can turn their heads three-quarters of a circle (270 degrees) in each direction. I've never seen an owl turn its head that far (and I've observed both wild and captive owls for hundreds of hours), so I'm skeptical of that claim. Mostly I see owls turn their heads up to 200 degrees, which is a little more than half a circle.

A few times I've observed an owl turn 220 degrees, but it never holds that pose for long.

So let's say an owl turns it head to the left 200 degrees. Now let's measure as the owl begins to turn back to the front and then proceeds to turn 200 degrees to the right. The owl has just turned its head 400 degrees of continuous movement. That covers more than a circle of movement, but that's not the same as turning its head all the way around.

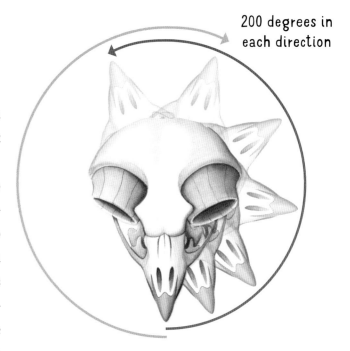

200 degrees in each direction

It may look like this Eastern Screech Owl is turning its head all the way around on its neck, but it really can't.

PREDATOR EYES

Most birds have eyes on the sides of their head (think robin or chickadee). Like you, however, owls view the world through forward-facing eyes. And like you, owls have **binocular vision**, which means that each eye sees a different version of what's in front of it. The brain overlaps the two versions, creating good depth perception and distance vision.

Unlike you, however, owls can't dart their eyes left or right, or roll them up or down, thanks to their eyes' tubular shape and a ring of bones (the sclerotic ring) that locks the eyes in place. To look away, an owl must turn its head, pivoting all 14 neck bones.

An old saying goes
"Eyes on the front, likes to hunt.
Eyes on the side, likes to hide."

OWL   ROBIN

■ Monocular   ■ Binocular

Predators such as owls have forward-facing eyes that focus better for catching prey. Prey animals have eyes more on the side of their heads so they can see predators sneaking up on them.

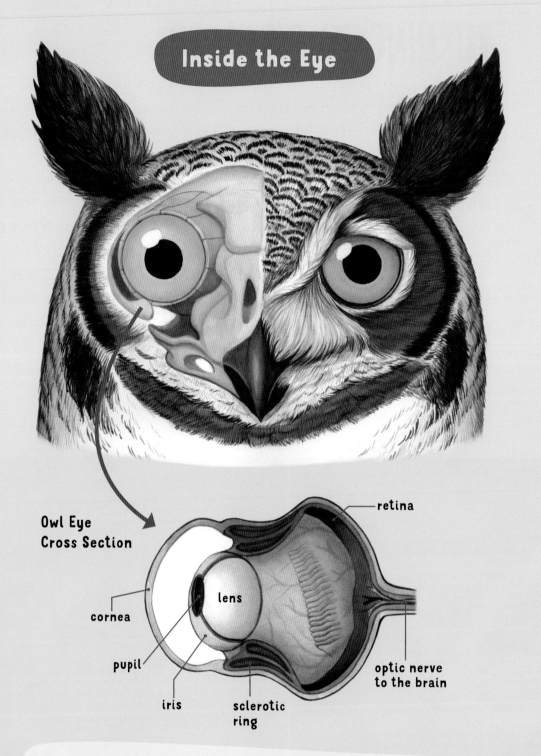

Inside the Eye

Owl Eye Cross Section

retina

cornea

lens

pupil

optic nerve to the brain

iris   sclerotic ring

See like an Owl

To see how binocular vision works:

1. Extend your arm and make a fist with your hand.

2. Point your thumb up.

3. Close your left eye while looking straight ahead at your thumb. Carefully notice what you can see.

4. Now open that eye, and without moving your head, close your right eye while still looking at your thumb.

Not exactly the same view, is it? Each eye takes in a slightly different picture of your world.

BLINK AND YOU'LL MISS IT

You have two eyelids on each eye, but an owl has three! In addition to upper and lower lids, owls have a translucent third eyelid, called a **nictitating membrane**, tucked out of sight near the beak. The upper eyelid is for blinking, the lower eyelid comes up for sleeping, and the nictitating membrane protects the eye, keeping it clean and moist.

Ever notice that pink bump in the corner of your eyes (closest to your nose)? Experts in anatomy say these are the remnants of a nictitating membrane our ancient ancestors had.

Upper eyelid   Lower eyelid   Nictitating membrane

With its nictitating membranes pulled across its eyes, this Barred Owl appears to have blue eyes.

Northern Hawk Owls

A mother owl feeding her active chicks often deploys her nictitating membranes to protect her eyes from a clumsy youngster's sharp beak.

Burrowing Owl

In flight, the nictitating membrane moistens and cleans the eyeball.

NIGHT VISION

How do owls see in the dark?
Having big, mushroom-shaped eyes is one way. Large eyes with big pupils allow more light in, enabling the owl to see details of a mouse in the shadows. If you were next to the owl as it watched a mouse in the dark, you'd be thinking, "What is that owl watching? I don't see anything."

Do owls see color? Humans see a large range of colors because our eyes have color-sensitive cells called *cones*. During the day, sunlight helps our cones detect color. Scientists think that owls have limited color vision because they have fewer cones in their eyes and more cells called *rods* that are sensitive to low light. At night, color becomes harder to see because cone cells don't work well in dim light.

Is seeing color important?
Does it matter to an owl if the mouse is gray or brown? No. Detecting movement and noticing details are more important for an owl hunting in the dark.

If you shine a flashlight toward an owl at night (or take a picture with a flash), it may seem to have glowing red eyes. What you're seeing is a reflection of light hitting the blood vessels at the back of the owl's eyes, creating those spooky orbs.

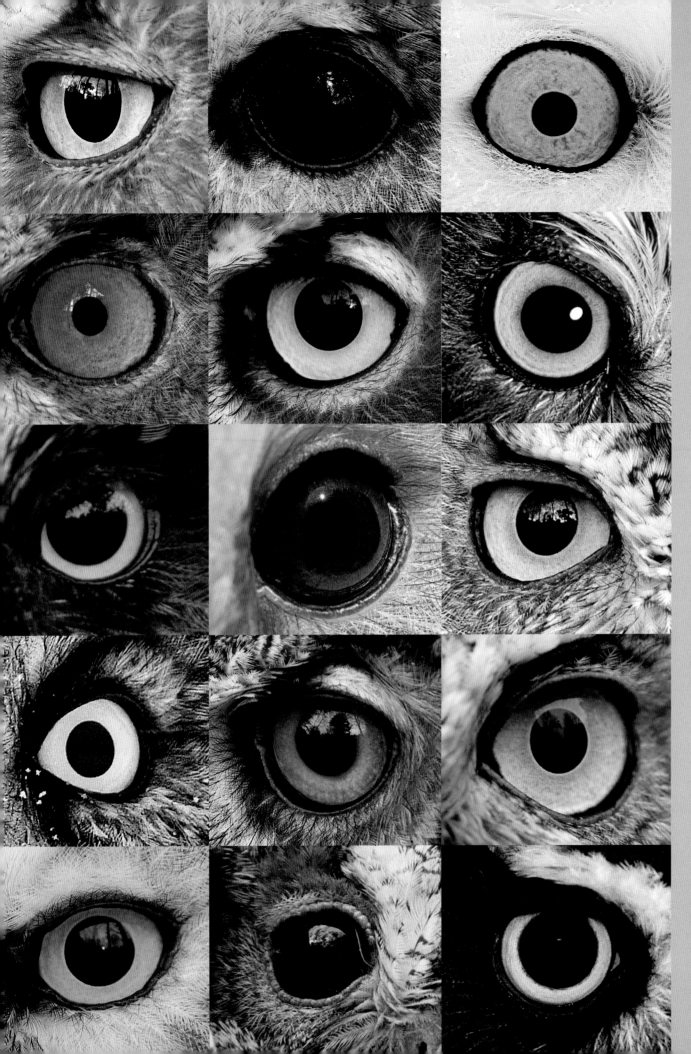

EYE COLOR

Owl eyes come in several colors, from the bright yellow eyes of the Great Horned Owl to the pumpkin-orange eyes of its close relative the Eurasian Eagle Owl (not a North American species), and from the dark brown eyes of the Barred Owl to the straw-colored eyes of an Eastern Screech-Owl.

Why do owls have different eye colors?

This seems like such a simple question! But I'm quick to admit that I don't know the answer, and neither do scientists. Some people claim that owls with such-and-such an eye color see better at night than owls with another eye color, but I've never found convincing experimental studies to back up these claims.

Top row: Eastern Screech-Owl (red morph), Barred Owl, Snowy Owl

2nd row: Eurasian Eagle Owl, Great Horned Owl, juvenile Northern Saw-whet Owl

3rd row: Short-eared Owl, Barn Owl, Eastern Screech-Owl (gray morph)

4th row: Great Gray Owl, Great Horned Owl (unusual blue color), Eastern Screech-Owl (gray morph),

Bottom row: Northern Saw-whet Owl, Flammulated Owl, Spectacled Owl

Hunting by Ear

Though owls catch their prey with their feet, it's their eyes and ears that guide those feet. We know that owls see well in low light, but what if a vole is rustling out of sight under fallen leaves or two feet of snow?

Good vision won't help secure supper then. Often an owl must rely on its hearing to exactly locate that vole before pouncing or plunging on it.

Owls have large ear openings that sit just behind the eyes. You can't see their ears because they are covered by feathers: very special feathers shaped like shallow saucers. These groups of feathers, called facial disks, form "sound funnels" around each ear.

If you gently peel back the ear flap, you can look into the owl's head and see where the eye socket disappears into the skull. (This is a captive owl.)

The facial disk, that circle of feathers around an owl's eyes, helps the owl hear better.

Hear like an Owl

To learn how facial disks work:

1. Place your cupped hands, palms facing forward, around your ears.

2. Swivel your head left and right, listening to what's happening around you. Zero in on a sound.

3. Drop your hands to compare your hearing without using them. Your cupped hands act as sound funnels. You'll hear sounds better using your handmade facial disks.

UNEVEN EARS

Most owls — Barred Owls, Great Horned Owls, screech owls and others — have symmetrical ears, meaning the openings are at the same height on each side of the head.

Other owls — Boreal Owls, Great Gray Owls, and Barn Owls — have asymmetric ears. That means one ear opening sits a little higher than the eyes, while the opposite ear opening sits a little lower than the eyes. This ear arrangement enables the owl to quickly and accurately locate very faint sounds.

Asymmetric ears work well because sounds strike each ear at slightly different times. If something rustles to the right of an owl, the sound hits the right ear about 30 millionths of a second before it strikes the left ear.

The owl turns its head to the right until the rustling sound hits both ears at the same time. Now the owl knows exactly where the sound is coming from. Time to pounce!

Researchers discovered that the Barn Owl's brain creates a map or mental picture of the space around a sound. The owl's brain has at least 95,000 neurons to process these "sound maps." Other birds, even really smart ones like crows, have about one-third of the neurons a Barn Owl has for hearing.

right ear flap

left ear flap

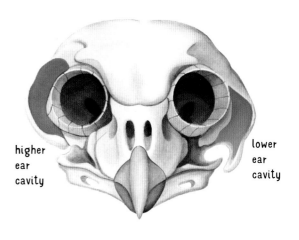

Asymmetric Ears

higher ear cavity

lower ear cavity

Owls use their hearing to pinpoint the soft sound of a mouse or vole digging under the snow.

ON SILENT WINGS

Many types of owls can fly without making any sound. Silent flight not only helps the owl sneak up on unsuspecting prey but also eliminates wing noise that might cover up the soft sounds made by a mouse or vole on the ground below.

Specialized feathers on the owl's wings cut through the air without creating noise. The leading edge of some wing feathers have serrations that create small turbulences. The top surfaces of these specialized feathers often feel like velvet or satin and have a sound-dampening effect.

The trailing edge of other feathers are fringed, looking almost like teeth on a comb. This structure muffles the sound of air moving across the wings. Fluffy body feathers on many kinds of owls further dampen sound from the wings.

NOT SO SILENT

The Great Gray Owl is perhaps the best example of a bird with soft body feathers that dampen sound. The Elf Owl, which lives in the hot, arid West, lacks the fluffy body feathers that dampen flight noise; this means that tiny Elf Owls might be noisier fliers than larger owls. Hmmm! That's interesting, because Elf Owls eat mostly insects and some insects can hear.

Surprisingly, owls don't fly silently all the time. When an owl is gliding, flying on the level, or descending, the flight is usually silent. A hovering owl can be silent. But when an owl grabs a weighty animal and takes off in labored flight, you will hear wing noise. At our **owlery**, we can hear Great Horned Owls when they fly steeply up from the ground to a perch.

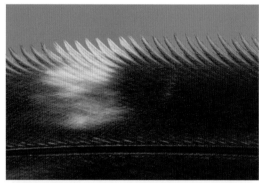

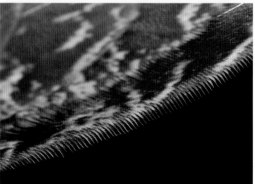

Above: Comblike serrations on owls' wing feathers make for quiet flight.

Left: A Short-eared Owl listens and watches for rodents as it hunts on a late afternoon.

TAKING THE PLUNGE

Hunting is hard work that takes a lot of time and energy. Locating and catching animals that are hidden under a thick layer of snow requires all of an owl's special talents. Watch how it's done, as this Great Gray Owl successfully nabs a vole.

Sitting high in a tree next to a snow-covered field, the owl looks and listens for movement. Hearing something under the snow, the owl launches into the air and hovers above the spot to pinpoint the location of its prey.

2 Suddenly it plunges headfirst into the soft snow.

3 The owl may make some jerky leg movements as it tries to grab the unseen rodent with its powerful feet and needle-sharp talons.

4 If it doesn't grab its prey immediately, the owl listens carefully to locate it.

5 Once the prey is secure, the owl transfers it from foot to beak.

6 The owl immediately swallows the prey in one gulp.

7 After a successful snack, the owl takes off to return to its perch to listen for another unlucky victim.

Specialized Feathers

Every feather on an owl serves a purpose. Some feathers have special jobs.

Alula feathers

Primary feathers

Secondary feathers

Facial disk feathers

Tail feathers

PRIMARY FEATHERS are the strong flying feathers. They are located on the outer wing. Some primaries have combed edges to help the owl fly silently.

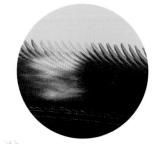

ALULA FEATHERS act like air brakes, helping a flying owl to slow down and drop onto a perch or prey.

TINY FACIAL DISK RUFF FEATHERS form the edge of the facial disk that cups an owl's eye like a saucer and focuses sound into the owl's ear.

"eyebrow" feather

DOWN FEATHERS work like long underwear. They keep the owl warm by trapping body heat next to the skin. If the owl gets hot, it flattens the down feathers so they don't trap heat.

TAIL FEATHERS are shaped differently from wing feathers, with more rounded ends. Owls use their tails to brake and turn.

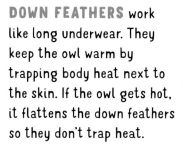

Bristles and hairlike feathers on an owl's head may help it detect flying insects in the dark.

Owls have feathered eyelids!

Ear tuft feathers can point backward, perhaps helping the owl pinpoint where a sound is coming from behind.

Frost coats the facial disks of this Barn Owl, who may be hunting during daytime in order to find enough to eat.

This Snowy Owl is cleaning and oiling its feathers, a process called preening.

Once a year, owls molt (shed) old, ragged feathers so that new ones can grow in. During this time, they can look a little funny.

Hunting with Hooked Feet

Owls are raptors: birds of prey that capture their food using strong feet equipped with sharp talons. They don't use their hooked beaks to catch animals. Instead, they use their beaks to rip their prey apart.

A strong adult human can exert about 140 pounds per square inch of pressure with his or her hand. Using its talons, a Great Horned Owl or a Eurasian Eagle Owl can out-squeeze a person. Though it's hard to measure, large owls probably exert more than twice the pressure of a human. The pressure from an owl pouncing on prey can be 300 times the owl's body weight, and the squeezing pressure at the tip of those needle-sharp talons is even greater!

Owls want to avoid getting bitten by their prey as it tries to escape, so they use their strong feet and sharp talons to kill the animal quickly. An owl usually grabs its prey by the head and neck. Sometimes the owl will sever the spinal cord in the neck or crush the skull of a struggling rodent with its powerful beak.

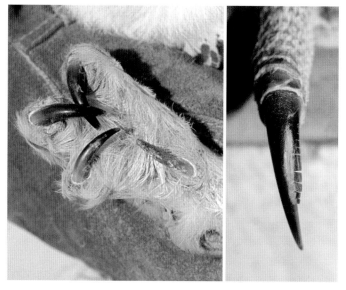

Talons are like human fingernails but are much narrower, sharper, and stronger.

Great Horned Owl

Z IS FOR ZYGODACTYL

Like most birds, owls have four toes on each foot. They have **zygodactyl** (zie-guh-DAK-til) feet, meaning that two toes point forward and two point backward. Unlike most other birds, however, owls have a special ability: they can swing one of their back toes to the front. With that movable toe, an owl can change its grip on wiggling prey. A few other birds, including ospreys, woodpeckers, and parrots, can do this as well.

Most other raptors — eagles, hawks, and falcons — have **anisodactyl** (an-i-so-DAK-til) feet, with three toes pointing forward and one toe pointing back. These raptors can't swing their fourth toe around like the owl does. That's too bad for them!

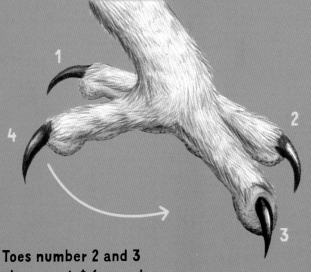

Toes number 2 and 3 always point forward. Toe number 1 always points backward. Toe number 4 is the movable one!

Snowy Owl tracks

CATCHING, THEN CACHING, PREY

An owl with prey usually carries it to a safe perch, off the ground, where it will eat its catch. A small rodent might be swallowed whole. Larger animals will be ripped open by the hooked beak. If the animal is a large one, the owl may **cache** (pronounced *cash*) some of it by tucking it in the fork of a branch and coming back to eat it, sometimes a day or two later. Most of the northern owls (Snowy Owl, Great Gray Owl, Northern Hawk Owl, Boreal Owl, Northern Saw-whet Owl) cache extra food.

Scientists think owls have good spatial memory, which means owls carry detailed mental maps of their surroundings. An owl's territory is often large, so it needs to remember where the hunting is good and where its nest or a favorite roost tree is. Locating cached food proves that owls have good memories.

Having eaten part of a duck, a Snowy Owl carries the rest of its meal to a safe place to cache (hide) it.

BEAKS TO FIT THE BILL

Birds don't have teeth like most other animals. Instead they have beaks. Beaks, sometimes called bills, come in lots of shapes and sizes to fit the ways different birds use them. Every bird has a beak that is best suited to its needs:

OWLS AND OTHER RAPTORS (hawks, eagles, falcons, kites) have sharp hooked beaks for tearing apart their prey. An owl's beak is always growing but is gradually worn down from use. After eating, an owl often wipes its beak clean on a branch or a stone.

A Burrowing Owl passes a grasshopper to its beak. Sometimes as parent owls fly back to the nest with a meal, they transfer their prey from their feet to their beaks to carry it. This allows them to easily land at the nest and quickly feed the hungry babies.

HAWKS use their pointed beaks to tear apart their prey.

Red-tailed Hawk

HUMMINGBIRDS probe flowers with their long, thin bills to find sweet nectar.

Hummingbird

Many **DUCKS** dabble in water for small insects, seeds, and plants. Diving ducks catch fish or pluck shellfish from underwater rocks.

Mallard Duck

FLAMINGOS turn their beaks upside down to filter algae, shrimp, and mollusks from the water. The upper bill is narrower than the lower one. It opens and closes the way the lower bill does in most birds.

Flamingo

BARN SWALLOWS catch insects on the wing with their gaping beaks.

Barn Swallow

CURLEWS probe in soft mud or earth to find worms and insects.

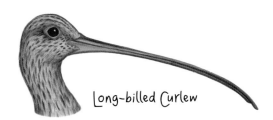

Long-billed Curlew

GOLDFINCHES have strong, cone-shaped beaks for cracking open hard seeds.

Goldfinch

CROWS have all-purpose beaks because they eat many different things.

Crow

FINDING A MATE

Most birds raise their chicks in the spring when it's warmer and food is easier to find, but many owls start courting in late winter or early spring.

Owls that live in the same area year-round are called **permanent residents**; they typically have the same mate for many years. **Migratory** owls spend winters away from the place they nest; they often have a different mate each breeding season.

Male owls announce and defend their territories by hooting or tooting. They also court the females with their calls. On a still, clear winter night, listen for the low, booming hoots of a Great Horned Owl. He's talking his mate into nesting for another year so that they can raise a new family of **owlets** (young owls). You may hear her calling back. Listen for their calls on an owl prowl.

Male and female Great Horned Owls hoot back and forth when they are courting. This male on the right is preening his mate's head feathers.

You can tell that this male Great Horned Owl is hooting because his throat feathers are all ruffled up and he's leaning forward.

FINDING A NEST

Owls don't build nests like many other birds do. Instead, they prefer to use an old stick or leaf nest built by another bird or mammal — maybe a hawk, a heron, an osprey, or even a squirrel. You could say owls are the original recyclers — smart indeed!

Some species of owls (nearly all the small owls) prefer to nest in cavities in trees, usually ones that have been excavated by woodpeckers, who used them for their nests. Certain owls prefer a natural cavity that might form when a large branch breaks off the tree and the wound rots, forming a hole.

Not all owls nest in trees. Burrowing Owls use old burrows of prairie dogs, gophers, armadillos, or tortoises. Sometimes a Great Horned Owl or Barn Owl female lays her eggs in the crotch of a tree, on a rock ledge, on the floor of a barn, or even on the bare ground.

Great Horned Owls often take over an abandoned Great Blue Heron nest and live peacefully with their much larger neighbors.

A pair of Barred Owl youngsters peer from their cavity nest in an oak tree. They'll soon be ready to explore their surroundings.

WHO LIVES WHERE?

Can you figure which owls use which kind of nest?
Read about the different species in chapter 2, then
see if you recognize them here.

Owls live all around!

Short-eared Owl in camouflaged ground nest 2 Barn Owl in a cave 3 Barn Owls in a nest box 4 Great Gray Owl in stick nest 5 Northern Hawk Owls in snag 6 Ferruginous Pygmy-Owl in saguaro cavity 7 Snowy Owl owlets in ground nest on the tundra 8 Burrowing Owls in abandoned prairie dog burrow

All about Owls   27

RAISING YOUNG

A female owl usually lays more than one egg, a day or two apart. Barn Owls might lay as many as a dozen eggs, though this is rare.

With most owls, after the female lays the first egg, she settles in to incubate the **clutch** (group) of eggs by sitting over them. A bare, featherless patch of skin on her belly, called a **brood patch**, allows her body heat to warm the eggs. Male owls don't have brood patches, so they don't incubate the eggs.

The mother owl rarely leaves the nest because she needs to keep the eggs warm and protected from egg-stealing predators like crows, ravens, magpies, and raccoons. The male goes out hunting for both of them and delivers meals to his mate as she sits on the eggs. If he is slow to bring supper, the female may screech-hiss a loud, complaining reminder that she's hungry.

A Barn Owl rolls her eggs before settling back onto them in a nest box.

A female Snowy Owl shelters her two-week-old chicks from the cold in their ground nest on the Arctic tundra.

FEEDING THE BABIES

Once the eggs hatch, the pressure is on the male to bring in even more food, so he may hunt night and day to secure enough food for his family. With most owls, the male hands off his catch to the female, who then rips up the prey and offers bits of meat to the tiny chicks, which are called owlets.

Young owls aren't shy about telling Mom and Dad they are hungry. They beg for food by screeching or hissing. This is a good sound to listen for from late spring through the summer, as it alerts you to the young owls in your neighborhood.

GROWING UP

After the chicks have grown up a bit, the female may leave them unattended and join in the hunt for food. As their feathers grow in, older babies stretch their wings and practice flapping, over and over. This builds their flight muscles and coordination. As the owlets get stronger, you might see their bodies start to lift off from the nest as they practice flapping. The owlets often look around in a surprised way when that happens!

The youngsters spend a lot of time looking at their new world, studying an insect crawling on a branch, a hawk flying overhead, or leaves moving in the breeze. Everything interests them. The owlets also spend hours preening

A male Long-eared Owl brings a mouse to his hungry mate, who will share it with their nestlings.

This egg and newly hatched Barn Owl babies are all from the same nest box. The female lays her eggs over several days, and they hatch in the order they were laid.

their feathers with their beaks. As their new adult feathers poke through, their downy baby feathers are slowly lost. The chicks often watch those baby feathers drift away on the breeze.

LEAVING THE NEST

Many owlets leave the nest before all their flight feathers are fully grown, a developmental stage called **branching**. They can't fly yet, so they often crash-land on the ground.

This is a dangerous time for the branchers. While they are on the ground, foxes, coyotes, Cooper's hawks, or other predators might catch them. Young forest owls that can't yet fly often climb well, using their strong feet and developing wings to "flap-climb" up a tree to safety. Here they wait for their parents to bring them meals of vole or flying squirrel.

By the time they are six or seven weeks old, most young owls are flying. Their flights are clumsy at first. If you are watching them, you might laugh or fret as they climb, fly, and crash into branches or bushes. You might not see the parent owls, but rest assured they are nearby keeping an eye on their youngsters.

A young Great Horned Owl tries to get the hang of flying. Landings can be a little rough.

Below: When Great Horned Owls first leave the nest, they can't fly very well, so they spend a lot of time sitting on branches waiting to be fed. This behavior is called branching.

FIRST FLIGHT

A young Barred Owl peers out of the nest box, then stretches its wings (1) and bursts into the air for a test flight (2). After a short rest on the forest floor (3), it flap-climbs back up the tree (4) and finds a safe spot to try again (5).

131

LOTS OF OWLETS

Fluffy baby owls don't look much like their parents, except for their round-eyed stares. See the owl profiles in chapter 2 to learn more about these youngsters.

ANSWER KEY: ❶ Burrowing Owl ❷ Snowy Owl ❸ Flammulated Owl ❹ Northern Saw-whet Owl ❺ Eastern Screech-Owl ❻ Great Gray Owl ❼ Great Horned Owl

GROWING UP

Among owls that don't migrate, like the Great Horned Owl, the young hang out with their parents for months, getting fed even after they are fully capable of catching their own food. Among migratory owls, the parents leave when their youngsters are a couple of months old and ready to fend for themselves.

Learning about the world is a dangerous business for these young owls. Bad weather, predators, accidents, food scarcities, and numerous other threats mean that as many as 85 percent of young owls die before they reach one year of age.

WHY MIGRATE?

While migration is risky for young owls, it's a strategy that allows birds to escape harsh winter conditions and come back to their breeding grounds in milder weather. Returning owls probably face less competition from other species of birds for food or nest sites than owls that don't migrate. It's a gamble, but the prize for migrating must be worth it, or else migratory species of birds wouldn't continue to thrive.

A young Great Horned Owl exercises its wings to strengthen the muscles it needs to fly.

>»2«<
Introducing the
OWLS

The sheer variety of owl species in the world boggles the mind. According to checklists created by **taxonomists** (scientists who study the relationships of different animals), at least 225 owl species inhabit the world, most of them occurring in tropical regions. Antarctica is the only continent that cannot claim any owls.

SCIENTIFIC NAMES

Humans have always tried to make sense of the seeming chaos of nature. Early on, this might have meant identifying which plants were good to eat and which plants were poisonous, or which animal might eat you. Later, to show how certain living things were related, people grouped together plants and animals that had similar qualities.

In the 1700s, a Swedish botanist named Carl Linnaeus (1707–1778) invented a system called **binomial nomenclature** that sorted all living things on Earth into increasingly specific groups: kingdom, phylum, class, order, family, genus, and species.

Each animal and plant is given a two-part scientific name that's derived from Greek or Latin. The first word is the genus, and the second word names the species.

Here's how the categories break down for a Great Horned Owl (*Bubo virginianus*).

KINGDOM:
Animal

PHYLUM:
Chordate
(All vertebrates)

CLASS:
Aves
(All birds)

ORDER:
Strigiformes
(All owls)

FAMILY:
Strigidae
(Owls other than Barn Owls)

GENUS:
Bubo
(Horned owls)

SPECIES:
virginianus
(Great Horned Owl)

Bubo means "horned owl" in Latin, and *virginianus* means "of Virginia."

OWLS OF NORTH AMERICA

Barn Owl
(page 38)

Drum roll, please! Allow me to introduce the 19 species of owls that breed and nest in the United States and Canada; some may be found in Mexico at times. Every state in America has owls, as do all of Canada's provinces and territories. Some owls found in North America are also found elsewhere in the world.

Some of "our" owls, such as the Great Horned Owl, are widespread and common. Others, such as the Ferruginous Pygmy-Owl and the Whiskered Screech-Owl, are found in specific locations and/or are much rarer.

Flammulated Owl
(page 42)

Western Screech-Owl
(page 44)

Eastern Screech-Owl
(page 46)

Whiskered Screech-Owl
(page 48)

Great Horned Owl
(page 50)

Northern Hawk Owl
(page 58)

Snowy Owl
(page 54)

Northern Pygmy-Owl (page 60)

Burrowing Owl (page 66)

Elf Owl (page 64)

Ferruginous Pygmy-Owl (page 62)

Spotted Owl (page 69)

Barred Owl (page 72)

Great Gray Owl (page 75)

Long-eared Owl (page 78)

Short-eared Owl (page 80)

Boreal Owl (page 82)

Northern Saw-whet Owl (page 84)

Barn Owl

Tyto alba   OLD NAMES: Monkey-Faced Owl, Church Owl, Belfry Owl, Ghost Owl

IDENTIFICATION

The Barn Owl is a medium-sized pale owl with a white heart-shaped face, dark eyes, and no ear tufts. It has long, nearly bare legs with thin bristles. Male Barn Owls are much whiter on the chest and belly than females. Females usually have gold coloring and more triangular spots on the chest, belly, and neck than males.

LENGTH: 15-21 INCHES

crow

WEIGHT: 0.7-1.3 POUNDS

WINGSPAN: 42-47 INCHES

Besides the Snowy Owl, Barn Owls are probably the most familiar and recognized owls in the world.

RANGE AND HABITAT

The Barn Owl is the world's most widely distributed owl, found on six continents, mostly in the warmer regions. It is missing from most of Canada, not found in Alaska, and rare or accidental across the northern tier of the United States except for Washington, where it is widely found at lower elevations. It was introduced to Hawaii in 1958.

Barn Owls don't survive well in cold, snowy climates. Severe winters can knock their population down drastically. Also, loss of grasslands to intensive agriculture and reforestation in the eastern United States means less **habitat** for Barn Owls, and their numbers are generally declining.

Year-round

VOICE

Barn Owls don't hoot. Instead, imagine a screech, scream, hiss, or other strange noise coming from a dark barn or cave. The screeches resemble the squeal of rubber car tires on pavement.

Might Be Mistaken For

In the bright glow of car headlights, a Barn Owl might be mistaken for a Barred Owl (page 72), since both can appear pale, have dark eyes, and lack ear tufts. However, Barred Owls are birds of the forest while Barn Owls are birds of farms and grasslands.

Barn Owls readily use nest boxes built for them.

NESTING BEHAVIOR

Unlike most other owl species, Barn Owls will breed any month of the year and typically produce two clutches a year with as many as nine eggs in a clutch. Sometimes a pair will raise a third clutch.

Barn Owls often roost or nest in old buildings (sometimes urban), barns, silos, sheds, steeples, cupolas, mine and well shafts, tree cavities, caves, and stacks of baled hay.

Bottom left: The female shreds regurgitated pellets with her feet to make a shallow nest to hold her eggs.

Bottom right: Barn Owls may reuse a nesting site for several breeding seasons.

Barn Owls nest in many different places, including, of course, barns! They are a good friend to farmers because they eat lots of rodents.

A Barn Owl brings a vole back to the nest. A breeding pair may stockpile prey animals around the nest while the eggs incubate so they'll have a supply of food for their hungry owlets.

SUPER SHARP EARS

Their proportionally small eyes suggest that Barn Owls rely on their hearing more than their eyesight to locate prey, and research indicates that Barn Owls may have the best hearing of any owls. In a study in which Barn Owls had their eyes covered, the owls caught prey using hearing alone. However, no owls are known to use echolocation to find prey like bats do.

HUNTING HABITS

Usually but not exclusively nocturnal, Barn Owls hunt over fields, grasslands, marshes, and desert, though they may roost in forest edges. In winter when food is scarce or when they are feeding multiple chicks, they may hunt during the day.

Barn Owls are common around agricultural areas, especially where pesticides aren't used. Some farmers put up nesting boxes to encourage Barn Owls to breed because an owl family can consume thousands of rodents in a year.

ON THE MENU

Barn Owls mostly hunt small rodents, especially rats, mice, voles, and lemmings. They also eat shrews, bats, and rabbits, and sometimes small birds such as starlings.

Voles

Mice

Shrews

Lemmings

Small birds

Chipmunks

Rats

Bats

Rabbits

Barn Owls, like all other raptors, may die if they eat rodents that have been poisoned. Widespread use of rodenticides in cities has caused declines in Barn Owl and other raptor populations.

Top: Downy baby feathers cling to the head of this Barn Owl.

Bottom: The beautiful spots of a Barn Owl remind some people of a starry night sky.

Flammulated Owl

Psiloscops flammeolus

IDENTIFICATION

The Flammulated Owl's dark eyes are a key identification, as all the other small owls in North America have irises with varying shades of yellow. It has ear tufts, but as these are often hard to see, the owl may appear round headed. It comes in gray and red **morphs**, with the red morph showing extensive **rufous** (reddish) feathers on the face and shoulders.

LENGTH:
6-6.75
INCHES

crow

WINGSPAN: 16 INCHES

WEIGHT: 1.6-2.2 OUNCES

The word *flammulated* means "having flame-shaped markings," and indeed the red streaks around the owl's eyes might look like small flames.

RANGE AND HABITAT

Flammulated Owls range widely in the mountains of the West, though they are hard to find because of their shy habits. They are not found in the East.

One of North America's most migratory owls, the Flammulated Owl winters in southern Mexico and Central America. Its summer habitat is high-elevation pine-fir-aspen forests. The sweet spot for nesting Flammulated Owls seems to be forests at elevations between 6,000 and 8,000 feet.

Breeding
Year-round
Nonbreeding
Migration

VOICE

The soft hoots of the Flammulated Owl can be hard to hear, though the owl may call more loudly when people aren't nearby. Rapid single- or double-noted hoots may continue for minutes on end during early breeding season.

Might Be Mistaken For

The Flammulated Owl could be confused with the Elf Owl (page 64) and the Western Screech-Owl (page 44), though neither of these two is common at the high elevations where the Flammulated Owl resides in summer, and neither has dark eyes. A Flammulated Owl is smaller than a Western Screech-Owl but larger than an Elf Owl.

Flammulated Owls nest in tree cavities made by woodpeckers and sapsuckers.

A RARE SIGHT

The first time you see a Flammulated Owl peering at you from the dark mountain forest, you might think you've spotted a forest gnome or an elf. The owl's dark eyes, studying you so intently, suggest other worlds that we humans hardly fathom. And like little gnomes or elves, the owls are always poised to dash into the forest, disappearing at the blink of an eye.

Trying to see a Flammulated Owl can be frustrating, even for experienced birders. This owl's restricted high-elevation breeding range, soft calls, shyness, and small size make for one elusive bird. (See Flammulated Owl Expert, page 115.)

An adult owl returns to its nest with a meal. Notice the band on its right leg.

A parent Flammulated Owl prepares to deliver a large ant to its chicks.

ON THE MENU

Flammulated Owls feed almost only on insects, especially moths, beetles, and grasshoppers. They hunt at night, picking their prey off of plants.

Beetles

Grasshoppers

Crickets

Spiders

Ants

Dragonflies

Moths

Western Screech-Owl

Megascops kennicottii   OLD NAME: Shivering Owl

IDENTIFICATION

Very similar to the Eastern Screech-Owl, the Western Screech-Owl has a blackish beak instead of the greenish/yellowish beak of its cousin. A stocky owl with ear tufts and straw-colored eyes, it is probably the most common owl in many parts of the West, though it's often overlooked. Its plumage is mostly gray, with a brown morph occurring in the Northwest. The red morph is rare.

LENGTH: 7.5-9.5 INCHES

WEIGHT: 3-10.5 OUNCES

crow

WINGSPAN: 18-22 INCHES

RANGE AND HABITAT

In Canada, the Western Screech-Owl is found in western and southern British Columbia and southwestern Yukon Territory. In the United States, it is found mostly west of the prairies, though its range overlaps with that of the Eastern Screech-Owl in parts of Texas.

It is found in low-elevation forests along waterways. This nonmigratory owl inhabits open woodlands, cottonwood trees along rivers, and trees around dwellings.

■ Year-round

VOICE

Recognizing the bouncing-ball call of the Western Screech-Owl is the best way to separate it from an Eastern Screech-Owl, which has a trill or whinny.

Might Be Mistaken For

The Western Screech-Owl is similar to the Eastern Screech-Owl (page 46) and the Whiskered Screech-Owl (page 48). Range maps coupled with elevation are a great help in figuring out which screech owl to expect in the area you are birding.

In the northern part of their range, they are found at elevations from sea level to about 3,000 feet. In New Mexico and Arizona, they occur at elevations up to 7,500.

Western Screech-Owls have dark beaks, while Eastern Screech-Owls have light greenish or yellowish beaks, though where the two ranges overlap, both screech owls may show greenish beaks.

Western Screech-Owl chicks leave the nest before they can fly.

BEHAVIOR

Like its eastern cousin, the Western Screech-Owl often lives in proximity to humans, roosting under eaves; in porches, sheds, or birdhouses; or among dense evergreens.

Western Screech-Owls nest in natural cavities, woodpecker-excavated cavities, and birdhouses. Nest sites are often reused year to year.

Females typically lay three or four eggs. Incubation lasts about a month. Owlets leave the nest 30 to 35 days after hatching.

Western Screech-Owls will eat just about anything they can catch, from insects (right) to birds nearly as big as themselves (above right).

ON THE MENU

Western Screech-Owls mostly hunt at night but may also hunt at dusk. They prey on a variety of animals and may tackle prey larger than themselves, including cottontail rabbits.

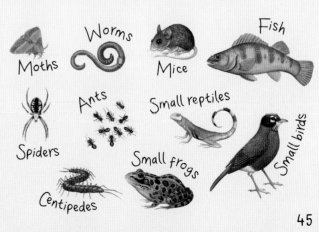

Moths Worms Fish Mice Spiders Ants Small reptiles Centipedes Small frogs Small birds

45

Eastern Screech-Owl

GRAY MORPH

RED MORPH

Megascops asio   OLD NAMES: Little Cat Owl, Little Horned Owl, Mottled Owl, Red Owl

IDENTIFICATION

The most common owl in many parts of the East, this small, chunky owl with ear tufts and straw-colored to bright yellow eyes is often overlooked. Note the pale greenish or bone-colored beak. The Eastern Screech-Owl comes in three morphs: red, brown, and gray. Gray morphs may be slightly more common than red morphs in the northern part of the range; red more common than gray in the southern part of the range.

WEIGHT: 3.3-9 OUNCES

LENGTH: 7.5-9.5 INCHES

crow

WINGSPAN: 18-22 INCHES

Screech-Owls like to sunbathe in the entrance to their roost.

RANGE AND HABITAT

The Eastern Screech-Owl is found widely throughout the East, though not at high elevations and not in most of Maine. It may also be found as far west as southeastern Saskatchewan, Montana, Wyoming, eastern Colorado, Oklahoma, and Texas. They are nonmigratory.

Year-round

VOICE

Eastern Screech-Owls rarely screech and usually only when in distress. The calls most often heard are a mellow **trill** and a descending **whinny** that sounds a bit like a horse. Watch and listen for scolding chickadees, nuthatches, titmice, blue jays, or other songbirds; such a group may have found a screech owl and are **mobbing** it, or trying to drive it away from their territory. Birders sometimes imitate a screech owl call to attract songbirds.

Might Be Mistaken For

Whiskered Screech-Owls (page 48) are similar in appearance but don't occur where Eastern Screech-Owls live. Western Screech-Owls (page 44) overlap the range of Eastern Screech-Owls in Mexico, Texas, and Wyoming, and interbreeding may occur there. In the overlap zone, identifying an Eastern Screech-Owl is best done by hearing the voice.

BEHAVIOR

Eastern Screech-Owls are widespread in suburban and urban settings where mixed forests with some older trees with cavities offer shelter for them to roost by day. They may also roost in birdhouses, under eaves and porch roofs, or in sheds.

Erecting nest boxes is a fine way of providing cavities in your yard or neighborhood.

Lots of people have heard an Eastern Screech-Owl (maybe without realizing what it was), but not so many people have seen one. When you hear its distinctive whinny or trill, look around carefully; the owl can't be far away.

Paired screech owls can be any combination of red and gray, as can the offspring. The color does not change through the life of the owl.

HUNTER AND HUNTED

Eastern Screech-Owls like to hunt along edges and in fields, lawns, parks, and wetlands. Larger raptors, including Barred and Great Horned Owls (pages 50 and 72), prey on Eastern Screech-Owls. The owls are also vulnerable to car strikes and rodenticides.

A friend who was cleaning out a nesting box found an interesting pellet with blue-and-yellow feathers. The owl had eaten an escaped parakeet!

Young screech owls often swallow small mice whole.

ON THE MENU

Eastern Screech-Owls hunt a variety of prey.

Spiders
Mice
Worms
Fish
Small reptiles
Small frogs
Centipedes
Songbirds
Pigeons
Crayfish
Salamanders
Snakes

Whiskered Screech-Owl

Megascops trichopsis   OLD NAME: Spotted Screech-Owl

IDENTIFICATION

A small, stocky owl with ear tufts and yellow eyes, the Whiskered Screech-Owl was named for the whiskerlike feathers sprouting around the beak and lower facial disks. These "whiskers" are almost impossible to see in the wild, making them a poor **field mark**. A rusty or buffy throat is another field mark. In the United States, only the gray morph occurs. In Mexico and Central America, where the owl is more common, a red morph is also found.

LENGTH: 6.5-8 INCHES

crow

WINGSPAN: 16-20 INCHES

WEIGHT: 2.5-3.5 OUNCES

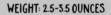

RANGE AND HABITAT

Birders make special trips to see this owl in the United States. It breeds only in the southeastern corner of Arizona and southwestern corner of New Mexico, where it is found in sky islands — forested, high-elevation mountains (4,000 to 8,200 feet) that rise steeply from the desert.

Year-round

The Whiskered Screech-Owl and the Western Screech-Owl can be hard to tell apart.

VOICE

The Whiskered Screech-Owl has a trilling song with fast, repeating notes sounding like **poo** or **boo**. It also may give a short **hoot**, **bark**, or **whistle**.

Might Be Mistaken For

The Whiskered Screech-Owl is very similar to the Western Screech-Owl (page 44) and may be impossible to separate by sight. Range and elevation, along with voice, will help you determine if the owl you are seeing is a Whiskered Screech-Owl.

Western Screech-Owls are about one third bigger than Whiskered Screech-Owls; however, the Whiskered's feet are larger than those of the Western.

The whiskers that give this owl its name are hard to see unless you can get a close view with binoculars or a telescope.

BEHAVIOR

Whiskered Screech-Owls often roost and always nest in cavities. These owls prefer evergreen oak, pine, and sycamore woods, often along canyon streams and washes.

They use natural cavities for nesting, rather than cavities excavated by woodpeckers, but they will also nest in birdhouses. Three eggs are an average clutch.

These screech owls often sunbathe in the cavity entrance, particularly after rain or a cool night. In addition to a cavity, a roost is often located at the base of a tree branch, up against the tree trunk, or on a branch surrounded by dense foliage.

If the nest cavity gets crowded and cramped with growing owlets, the female may sit in the entrance all day.

ON THE MENU

Whiskered Screech-Owls prey heavily on insects (including caterpillars) and also take spiders, centipedes, lizards, snakes, small birds, bats, shrews, and rodents.

In Arizona, the diet of Whiskered Screech-Owls shifts from mostly moths and caterpillars in early summer to june bugs and other beetles in late June and July, when the monsoon rains cause beetle numbers to swell.

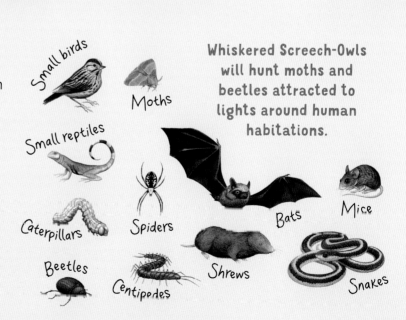

Whiskered Screech-Owls will hunt moths and beetles attracted to lights around human habitations.

Small birds
Moths
Small reptiles
Caterpillars
Spiders
Bats
Mice
Beetles
Centipedes
Shrews
Snakes

Great Horned Owl

Bubo virginianus   OLD NAMES: Big Cat Owl, Hoot Owl

IDENTIFICATION

The Great Horned Owl's large size, long ear tufts, and bright yellow eyes with black pupils make it fairly easy to identify. Great Horned Owls vary widely in coloration. Those in the East are the most colorful, with rufous facial disks and black **barring** overlying rufous belly feathers. Great Horned Owls of the **boreal** northern forest of central Canada show no brown or rufous coloring, overall looking black and white. In parts of the West, the owls may appear grayer than their colorful eastern counterparts.

LENGTH: 18-26 INCHES

crow

WEIGHT: 1.6-5.5 POUNDS

WINGSPAN: 38-60 INCHES

RANGE AND HABITAT

The Great Horned Owl is North America's most widespread owl. It is found in all states except Hawaii; north to the tree line in Canada and Alaska; and southward into Mexico. It is also found in Central America and many parts of South America.

Year-round
Year-round (scarce)

Great Horned Owls are the only owl to regularly eat skunks!

VOICE

Listen for the five-noted hoots of the Great Horned Owl in winter when the owls are courting. Heard from afar, the call may sound like four notes. Some people think the call sounds like Who's awake? Me, too! Great Horned Owl calls carry well through the woods, and can often be heard from quite a distance.

Although some birders claim to use the pitch of the Great Horned Owl's call to tell males from females, doing so is tricky. During winter courtship, the male makes a low-pitched booming hoot. Later in the season, the pitch of the male's hoots may go up and sound more like the higher-pitched hoots of a female.

Laying eggs in the winter means the female may incubate them while falling snow blankets her back.

Might Be Mistaken For

The Long-eared Owl (page 78) resembles the Great Horned Owl in feather color, eye color, ear tufts, and perching habits. However, Long-eared Owls are smaller and slimmer than Great Horned Owls and have streaking on the chest and belly. Great Horned Owls have chest and belly barring.

You're more likely to see a Great Horned Owl, as Long-eared Owls are not only scarce but also hard to find because they roost in dense bushes or trees, sometimes high up.

BEHAVIOR

Other than the Barn Owl, which will nest any month of year, the Great Horned Owl is the earliest owl to nest in North America, even in northern climates. Midwinter courtship is quickly followed by egg laying.

Great Horned Owls often reuse a stick nest built by other large birds. Sometimes they nest in the crotch of a tree. They also nest in tree hollows, caves, cliff ledges, barns, and (rarely) hollow logs on the ground. One unusual desert pair nested on the bare earth under a tree in a schoolyard in southeastern Arizona.

The female lays on average two or three eggs. The male brings her food while she is on the nest.

Once the chicks are hatched, the female stays with them, protecting them from harsh weather and predators like raccoons and hawks, while the male continues delivering food for the female to feed their young.

When the chicks are a few weeks old, the mother joins the hunt and brings in food along with the male.

While nesting, Great Horned Owls contend with winter cold and snow in temperate areas, and with brilliant sun and hot days in desert areas. The female will shade young owlets with her body and wings to keep them cool. Panting Great Horned Owl owlets are a common sight in nests that aren't shaded.

Great Horned Owls will defend their nests fiercely by hooting, hissing, grunting, and screaming.

51

Great Horned Owl *continued*

It's deep winter in New England and this big female Great Horned Owl is probably getting ready to nest. Across North America, Great Horned Owls are the first birds to nest each year (though Barn Owls lay eggs any month of the year).

Owlets leave the nest before they are able to fly well. Sometimes their first attempts end in crash landings, but the determined youngster shakes it off and keeps trying.

ATTRACTING A MOB

One of the easiest ways to locate a Great Horned Owl is to listen for noisy crows. If a crow happens to spot a sleeping Great Horned Owl in a pine tree, the crow lets loose with an alarm call, alerting other crows to the owl in the neighborhood. Soon 10, 20, or more crows may surround the tree, cawing and wheeling about.

This behavior is called mobbing. The crows know that Great Horned Owls can prey on them, particularly at night when the crows are sleeping. So to make their neighborhood safer, they mob the owl, attempting to drive it off.

ON THE MENU

Great Horned Owls prey on a wide variety of animals: bats, rodents, skunks, fish, frogs, snakes, small owls, crows, and other birds. They will attack small cats and occasionally small unattended dogs. This is the only owl to regularly prey on skunks. A starving Great Horned Owl may attempt to take a porcupine, usually with dire results for the owl.

Fish

Crows

Skunks

Songbirds

Mice

Snakes

Pigeons

Small owls

Small frogs

Bats

Shorebirds

Chipmunks

Voles

Snowy Owl

Bubo scandiacus   OLD NAMES: White Owl, Arctic Owl

IDENTIFICATION

Plumage varies widely from nearly pure white to very dark, with heavy chest barring and spotting against white feathers. Snowy Owls have tiny ear tufts that are usually not visible. The feet are fully feathered, even on the bottoms.

WEIGHT: 2.9-5.9 POUNDS

LENGTH: 20-27 INCHES

crow

WINGSPAN: 49-57 INCHES

RANGE

Snowy Owls nest on the Arctic tundra in summer in northern Alaska and Canada as well as northern Europe and Asia. The Pacific Northwest, the northern tier of states, New England, and most of southern Canada see Snowy Owls most winters.

Breeding
Year-round
Winter
Irruptive

VOICE

Snowy Owls are not very vocal in winter. On Arctic nesting territory, the male's rough-sounding groooo or broooo carries across the tundra. Migratory Snowy Owls may cackle in winter in response to a harassing peregrine falcon or another Snowy Owl competing for food, sounding like kuk-kuk-kuk or kack-kack-kack.

Might Be Mistaken For

Great Horned Owls (page 50) of the far north appear black and white, wearing none of the rufous or brown plumage of their southern kin. These colorless Great Horned Owls could be confused with a Snowy Owl.

This large, powerful bird with its striking yellow-and-black eyes is North America's most recognizable owl.

Above: This male Snowy Owl, still slightly damp from a bath, has a pure white plumage with no dark markings. The brown coloration on the belly is soiled feathers.

ON THE MOVE

Snowy Owls sometimes move southward in the fall in great numbers in unpredictable years, a movement called **irruption**. Some years Snowy Owls travel to Texas, Oklahoma, Arkansas, Florida, Hawaii, and Bermuda.

It used to be thought that the owls moved south because they were starving, but recent research indicates that an irruption of Snowy Owls echoes a successful nesting season in the Arctic the previous summer. Many of the Snowy Owls that fly south are first-year birds.

Snowy Owls often perch on the ground in open areas, as well as on rooftops, fence posts, telephone poles, dune tops, jetties, haystacks, barns and silos, airport structures, pack ice, and stand-alone trees.

NESTING BEHAVIOR

If you are lucky enough to observe Snowy Owls at their nest in the Arctic in June or July, it's easy to tell who the mother is: she's the one incubating the eggs and protecting the downy chicks from cold, wet weather. The male brings food to her as she tends the eggs and broods the chicks. Male Snowy Owls are known to aggressively defend their nest against human intruders.

Bird guides and birders often claim that a pure white Snowy Owl with no black markings is a male, but this isn't a reliable field mark. An owl breeder in Ontario had a pure white Snowy Owl in captivity that turned out to be a female!

Snowy Owl *continued*

HUNTING HABITS

Snowy Owls hunt on the wing. Unlike other owls, Snowy Owls sometimes soar, using thermals (updrafts of air) to climb higher and float in the air.

Some breeding Snowy Owls stay in the Arctic all winter and may spend time on the sea ice hunting sea ducks that concentrate in openings in the ice called polynyas.

A Snowy Owl was seen chasing a pomarine jaeger (a large predatory bird that seems part gull, part raptor) across the Arctic tundra, forcing it to drop a lemming it had caught. The owl snatched the falling lemming out of midair with its powerful feet!

The owl tears apart larger prey, like this gull, to eat it . . .

ON THE MENU

Snowy owls eat ducks, geese, gulls and other shorebirds, great blue herons, American kestrels, Short-eared Owls (page 80), sparrows, lemmings, rats, voles, mice, and even cats.

A Snowy Owl was spotted eating another Snowy Owl at Boston's Logan Airport!

Gulls

Mice

Lemmings

Ducks

Shorebirds

Short-eared Owls

Voles

Sparrows

Kestrels

Rats

Great blue heron

. . . but swallows smaller animals, like this vole, whole.

The Snowy Owl is North America's fastest owl, clocking flight speeds of more than 60 miles per hour.

Northern Hawk Owl

Surnia ulula   OLD NAMES: American Hawk Owl, Day Owl

IDENTIFICATION

A fast-flying, medium-sized owl with somewhat pointed wings and a long tail, the Northern Hawk Owl is heavily barred on its chest and belly. Its yellow-and-black eyes are framed by facial disks edged thickly with black. In proportion to body size, it has the smallest feet and shortest legs of any North American owl. Its actions and habits are reminiscent of an Accipiter hawk, hence the word *Hawk* in its name.

LENGTH: 14–17.5 INCHES

crow

WEIGHT: 0.6–1.0 POUND

WINGSPAN: 28–35 INCHES

RANGE AND HABITAT

A resident of the boreal forest, the Northern Hawk Owl occasionally irrupts (moves) southward out of Canada and Alaska into the northern states. These irruptions often parallel those of Great Gray Owls, since both species rely heavily on red-backed voles for food. They may linger for days in an area where winter prey is abundant.

Year-round

Winter Irruption

VOICE

The Northern Hawk Owl is rarely heard outside its nesting area, but winter birders might hear an alarm call — a rapid **creek-creek-creek** — if the owl interacts with other raptors.

On the nesting grounds, the courtship call is a rapid trilling of **popopopopopo** or **lulululululu** notes, usually given at night.

Might Be Mistaken For

The Northern Hawk Owl is more likely than any other species of owl to be mistaken for a hawk. Its fast, direct style of flight is like that of a Cooper's hawk, which it resembles in size, though the hawk doesn't have the bulky head of the Northern Hawk Owl.

When the Northern Hawk Owl is perched, its feet and legs are hidden beneath fluffy belly feathers.

BOLD BIRDS

Seeming unafraid of people, a Northern Hawk Owl may fly close to them or perch nearby, studying its human admirers with an intense stare. This owl surveys large fields and open areas when hunting, and can rapidly cover large distances in short bursts of flight.

Northern Hawk Owls can often be spotted perched on the top tip of evergreen trees, telephone poles, or roof peaks, where they have an expansive view of fields for hunting.

Top left: Can you find all six of the baby Northern Hawk Owls huddled in their snag nest?

Top right: Northern Hawk Owls hunt primarily by sight during daylight. This one has caught a partridge.

NESTING BEHAVIOR

Northern Hawk Owls frequently nest in cavities or atop snags in recently burned spruce forest. They may be mobbed by Bonaparte's gulls in areas where the gulls also nest in spruce trees.

These owls find a different mate every breeding season. They tend to be solitary when not raising a family.

In flight, a Northern Hawk Owl can look more like a hawk than an owl, but don't be fooled.

ON THE MENU

Usually hunting by day, this fast-flying owl preys primarily on voles and other rodents, though it will take prey as large as a partridge, grouse, or young snowshoe hare.

Squirrels

Partridges

Snowshoe hares

Mice

Voles

Lemmings

Northern Hawk Owls often cache excess food by tucking it into the crotch of a tree, going back to feed later.

Northern Pygmy-Owl

Glaucidium gnoma

IDENTIFICATION

This small, round-headed owl with a spotted crown has yellow eyes with black pupils and blackish streaks on its belly. The tail is banded with white or light brown bars.

WEIGHT: 1.3–2.6 OUNCES

LENGTH: 6.5–7.3 INCHES

crow

WINGSPAN: 12–15 INCHES

The Northern Pygmy-Owl hunts by day or night.

RANGE

Northern Pygmy-Owls are found in southeastern Alaska, the southern two-thirds of British Columbia, southwestern Alberta, and most of the western United States. They are largely absent from Nevada and found only in western Montana and Colorado. In the Rocky Mountains, these owls move to lower elevations in winter. It's not known if other populations migrate north to south in fall.

Year-round

VOICE

A series of one-note whistled toots.

Might Be Mistaken For

A key field mark for the Northern Pygmy-Owl is the spotted crown. Compare it with the streaked crown of the Ferruginous Pygmy-Owl (page 62).

All pygmy owls have false "eyes" or "eye spots" on the back of the head. It's possible that the spots fool attackers into thinking that the owl is watching them.

Like all small owls, Northern Pygmy-Owls prefer to nest in tree cavities.

Above left: The Northern Pygmy-Owl watches for prey from a high spot. When it spots something, it drops headfirst before spreading its wings.

BEHAVIOR

This owl is hard to find and observe during the breeding season. It inhabits a mixed forest of conifers or oaks.

Northern Pygmy-Owls are cavity nesters and will sometimes reuse a nest from the previous year. Females lay on average four or five eggs and incubate them for about 28 days. At about 9 or 10 days, the female starts to leave the nest and join the hunt.

Northern Pygmy-Owls are active by day and into the twilight and probably at night, though this is not well documented.

These little owls are fierce hunters, sometimes taking prey more than twice their own weight.

ON THE MENU

Northern Pygmy-Owls mostly prey on small birds, such as hummingbirds, warblers, chickadees, and sparrows, but they eat a wide variety of other animals as well.

Shrews   Mice   Beetles
Small reptiles   Moths
Chipmunks   Voles
Dragonflies   Sparrows

Because they will sometimes raid nests of other birds to grab nestlings, other birds will mob a Northern Pygmy-Owl to drive it away.

Ferruginous Pygmy-Owl

Glaucidium brasilianum

IDENTIFICATION

A small, round-headed owl with a streaked crown, the Ferruginous Pygmy-Owl has yellow eyes with black pupils and brown streaks on its belly. It has the false "eyes" or "eye spots" that all pygmy owls display (see the Northern Pygmy-Owl on page 60). The tail is banded with rufous bars.

WEIGHT: 1.6-3.6 OUNCES

LENGTH: 6.75-7.5 INCHES

crow

WINGSPAN: 12 INCHES

RANGE AND HABITAT

This nonmigratory species is much more widespread and common in Mexico and Central and South America than in North America.

It inhabits a small range in the Sonoran Desert in south-central Arizona, where it is usually found breeding at elevations between 1,000 and 4,300 feet in saguaro-paloverde scrub desert and in paloverde-mesquite uplands.

In southern coastal Texas, it breeds in oak-mesquite forests and forests near streams and washes.

Year-round

VOICE

These owls often call during the cooler part of the day, giving a quick series of whistled toots. A vocalizing Ferruginous Pygmy-Owl risks attention from birds such as vireos, warblers, gnatcatchers, woodpeckers, and wrens, who may mob the tiny owl to drive it away.

The word *ferruginous* (fer-RU-gin-us) means "rust colored" and refers to the reddish bands on the tail.

Might Be Mistaken For

Compare the Ferruginous Pygmy-Owl with the Northern Pygmy-Owl (page 60), which has a spotted crown rather than a streaked one. The tail on a Ferruginous Pygmy-Owl is noticeably rufous or orange-brown compared with the dark brown-and-white bars on the Northern Pygmy-Owl tail.

The Ferruginous Pygmy-Owl has a highly restricted range compared with the wide range of the Northern Pygmy-Owl, so the location will help you figure out which one it is.

Above: An adult owl peers out of its nesting site in a saguaro cactus.

Below: The male brings food to his mate and nestlings for the first three weeks after they hatch.

BEHAVIOR

Ferruginous Pygmy-Owls average three to five eggs in a clutch. Incubation runs for 26 to 28 days in Texas nests. The father brings small prey like lizards and insects to the nest in his beak and carries larger prey with his feet.

Snakes may be a major predator of pygmy owl eggs in Texas. Raccoons prey on eggs or chicks in the nest. As in many places and with many species of small owls, Cooper's hawks and Great Horned Owls prey on adults and fledglings.

ON THE MENU

In some locations, these owls primarily eat large insects, such as grasshoppers, scorpions, and caterpillars. Bold daytime hunters, they may attack animals bigger than they are, such as lizards and quail.

Wood rats

Grasshoppers

Crickets

Mice

Wrens

Small reptiles

Scorpions

Moths

Elf Owl

Micrathene whitneyi

IDENTIFICATION

Less than 6 inches tall, the Elf Owl is the smallest owl in the world. It has yellow-and-black eyes, no ear tufts, a short tail, and no eye spots on the back of the head. Elf Owls look slender and don't fluff out like screech owls often do. Females often show more rufous coloring on the face and upper chest than the grayer males.

WEIGHT: 1.3–1.7 OUNCES

LENGTH: 5.25–5.75 INCHES

crow

WINGSPAN: 12–14 INCHES

RANGE AND HABITAT

The Elf Owl is restricted in the United States to southern parts of Arizona, New Mexico, Texas, and (rarely) southeast California.

It is comfortable in diverse habitats, including mesquite and paloverde trees along desert washes, mountain pine-oak forests, oak forests, and forests along rivers and canyon bottoms.

Breeding
Year-round
Nonbreeding
Migration

This tiny owl is about the size of a sparrow.

VOICE

This tiny owl has an unexpectedly loud voice. Calls include a surprising variety of barks, squeaks, and whistles. Its defensive call is a rapid series of barks. The song is a series of squeaky or nasal pee-pee-pee-pee-pee notes.

Might Be Mistaken For

Compare the Elf Owl with the Northern Pygmy-Owl (page 60) and the Ferruginous Pygmy-Owl (page 62). Elf Owls lack the false eye spots that the pygmy owls have on the backs of their heads.

CAVITY NESTER

Elf Owls roost and nest in cavities in trees, utility poles, and saguaro cacti (in the Sonoran desert) excavated by woodpeckers and flickers. Nesting territories can be small if insect prey is abundant. Elf Owl pairs may nest surprisingly close together in good habitat with lots of prey.

As is true with most cavity-nesting owls, Elf Owls lay their eggs on the cavity floor. No nesting material is brought into the chamber.

On average, three to four eggs are laid. The female incubates the eggs for about 24 days. Once hatched, the owlets stay in the nest for about a month.

After the hot season passes, Elf Owls will roost in trees and thickets as well as cavities.

Top: Talons are useful for landing as well as hunting.

Right: The male often roosts in the nest cavity with the female, which must make for cramped quarters.

BEHAVIOR

Elf Owls are **crepuscular**, which means they are most active around dawn and dusk, though their activity extends well into the night.

On a summer day, you might spy an Elf Owl peeking at you from the cool, shaded depths of its nest cavity. Sometimes, all you get is a quick glimpse of half its face and one dimly lit eye studying you before the owl ducks out of sight.

If the cavity is in a saguaro, the thick cactus walls that enclose the cavity probably insulate the owls from summer's hot daytime temperatures.

ON THE MENU

Elf Owls mostly eat insects, including crickets, grasshoppers, beetles, and moths, often hunting them on the wing. Sometimes they take scorpions, small snakes, and lizards.

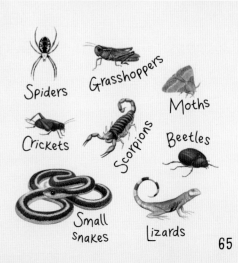

Spiders Grasshoppers Moths Crickets Scorpions Beetles Small snakes Lizards

Burrowing Owl

Athene cunnicularia

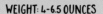

IDENTIFICATION

This small, long-legged owl of open grasslands and desert is often seen perching on the ground or on low fence posts, mounds, and bushes. It has yellow eyes, a barred belly, a spotted back, and a white throat patch but no ear tufts.

WEIGHT: 4–6.5 OUNCES

LENGTH: 9–11 INCHES

crow

WINGSPAN: 22–24 INCHES

RANGE AND HABITAT

Burrowing Owls have two distinct populations: a nonmigratory one in southern Florida and one in the West that is migratory in the northern part of the range.

The species is endangered in southern Alberta, Saskatchewan, and Manitoba, Canada.

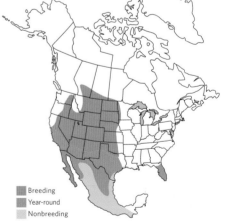

Breeding
Year-round
Nonbreeding

Burrowing Owls are unusual among owls and other birds in that they live underground. They are also unusual because the males and females are the same size. Female raptors of most species are larger than males.

Burrowing Owls are active day and night, but they often spend the hottest part of the day in the shade of bushes or grass clumps, or underground in their burrows.

VOICE

The male's song is cu-cuhooh or coo-cooo. Both adults and young have a large range of smooth-sounding musical notes. When feeling threatened in its burrow, a Burrowing Owl gives a call that sounds like a rattlesnake vibrating its tail. That's a sound that might give a predator cause to pause!

These animated little owls often bob their heads when curious or upset. Youngsters may peer at you with their faces turned upside down.

BEHAVIOR

The only owl in the world to regularly nest underground, the Burrowing Owl in the West is often associated with prairie dogs, whose unused burrows it nests in. In Florida, Burrowing Owls use burrows dug by armadillos and gopher tortoises. They will use buried nest boxes and can be found in grasslands, airports, agricultural areas, golf courses, and housing developments.

The burrows can extend several feet into the ground. The nest may be lined with animal dung, feathers, grass, or other materials. The female lays from two to twelve eggs, which she incubates for about 30 days.

Right: When the desert sand is hot, a run to the shade is in order for this owl.

Burrowing Owl *continued*

An adult Burrowing Owl carries a grasshopper back to its hungry chicks at the nest burrow. Note the metal band on its left leg, which identifies the owl and allows researchers to study individual birds.

This adult has captured a glass lizard near its Florida burrow. Glass lizards are often mistaken for snakes as they have no legs.

ON THE MENU

Burrowing Owls hunt any time of day and prey on a large number of species. Females hunt more by day, mostly for insects, while males hunt more at night and catch small animals.

Beetles

Small frogs

Voles

Salamanders

Mice

Small lizards

Shrews

Worms

Spiders

Caterpillars

Grasshoppers

Dragonflies

Snakes

Small birds

Scorpions

Moths

Crickets

Spotted Owl

Strix occidentalis

IDENTIFICATION

This medium-sized owl has dark eyes set in a large, rounded head with no ear tufts. The beak is yellowish green. The upper chest has some dark barring, while the belly has a combination of bars and spots.

The three subspecies are the Northern Spotted Owl, the California Spotted Owl, and the Mexican Spotted Owl. The Northern is the darkest brown and the Mexican the lightest brown of the three, though separating a Northern from a California Spotted Owl would be tricky at best.

LENGTH: 17-19 INCHES

crow

WINGSPAN: 42-44.5 INCHES

WEIGHT: 1.1-1.7 POUNDS

RANGE AND HABITAT

Found as far north as southwest British Columbia, the Spotted Owl is also present in shaded forest canyons of Arizona, New Mexico, Utah, Colorado, and a small region in West Texas.

A threatened species, it is disappearing in parts of California and the Pacific Northwest because of old-growth-forest logging, development, and habitat fragmentation.

Year-round

VOICE

The Spotted Owl's three-part hoot — hoo-hoo, hoooo with a pause between the second and third syllables — is mostly heard at night.

Might Be Mistaken For

The Spotted Owl resembles the Barred Owl (page 72), which has a barred chest and a streaked belly, in contrast to the Spotted Owl's bars and spots on the belly. The range of the Barred Owl overlaps that of the Spotted Owl in California, Oregon, Washington, and British Columbia.

An ample pile of whitewash (bird poop) under a tree, along with at least a few pellets, can be a clue to a favorite day roost. During the summer, Spotted Owls often roost quite low in the cooler shaded understory.

Spotted Owl *continued*

A fledgling Spotted Owl enjoys its dinner of wood rat, right down to the long tail.

NESTING BEHAVIOR

Spotted Owls usually nest in tree cavities or at the tops of snags, or in stick nests constructed by other large birds, or sometimes in mistletoe brooms or tree crotches. The Mexican Spotted Owl, more than the other subspecies, nests on cliff ledges, though it frequently uses stick nests and cavities.

Pairs of owls form a bond over many years and live in a home territory. They often roost near their future nest site for a few weeks in advance of mating and laying eggs.

Females lay one to four eggs, usually two. The female incubates the eggs for about a month, during which time the male delivers food to her at the nest. The female stays with the chicks for the first 10 days or so, brooding them and feeding them.

After that, the female begins to join the hunt and both parents will bring in prey and feed it to the young. The young typically leave the nest about 35 days after hatching.

Predators of Spotted Owls include Great Horned Owls, northern goshawks, Cooper's hawks (preying on fledglings), and fishers (large relatives of the weasel). Common ravens have been known to steal eggs.

ON THE MENU

Northern Spotted Owls prey mostly on flying squirrels, wood rats, voles, snowshoe hares, rabbits, and pocket gophers; they also prey, though less so, on frogs, songbirds, small owls, and insects. Important prey for **California Spotted Owls** are flying squirrels and wood rats with mice, moles, squirrels, and insects taken in smaller amounts. **Mexican Spotted Owls** favor mice, voles, rabbits, and bats.

When prey is plentiful, Spotted Owls will cache food on mossy limbs, in the tops of snags, in nooks at the base of trees, or among rocks.

Flying squirrels — Mice — Moles — Wood rats — Voles — Small owls — Small frogs — Cottontail rabbits — Crickets — Pocket gophers — Songbirds — Bats

A pair of Spotted Owls will often roost together on the same limb, day after day, occasionally awakening to preen each other's heads.

Barred Owl

IDENTIFICATION

A dark-eyed, big-headed owl with large facial disks, it gets its name from bars on the upper chest. The belly has vertical stripes. It has no ear tufts.

LENGTH: 17-24 INCHES

crow

WEIGHT: 1-2.3 POUNDS

WINGSPAN: 40-50 INCHES

The Barred Owl is probably the second most common owl in many parts of the East, after the Eastern Screech-Owl (page 46).

RANGE

Barred Owls are found in the East, the Pacific Northwest, and the southern Canadian provinces.

■ Year-round

EXPANDING TERRITORY

Barred Owls arrived in the West perhaps 100 years ago, but in the last few decades they are causing the endangered Spotted Owl real problems. In the Pacific Northwest, they are outcompeting them for food. They also breed with Spotted Owls (page 69), creating hybrids sometimes called "Sparred" Owls. In some forests, Spotted Owls have disappeared altogether, replaced by the larger, more aggressive Barred Owls.

Might Be Mistaken For

Many people confuse the similar-sounding names of Barred and Barn Owls (page 38). The Barn Owl also has dark eyes and no ear tufts and can be quite noisy, though its calls are noticeably different. Barn Owls have a distinctive bright white, heart-shaped face, whereas a Barred Owl's grayer face has two unequal half circles around the eyes.

Though they have similar weights, Barn Owls look skinny while Barred Owls look plump because of their thick, fluffy feathers. Barn Owls have no barring on the chest and no stripes on the belly.

Top right: Owls often stretch wings and legs after perching for long periods. Sometimes a stretch tells you they are getting ready to fly.

Top left: Barred Owls are often mobbed (attacked) by smaller birds, like this blue jay, who call and dive-bomb the predator to draw attention to it and drive it away.

VOICE

If you think you're hearing a monkey in the woods, it's probably a Barred Owl. The classic eight-note hoot is popularly described as sounding like Who cooks for you? Who cooks for you all? The call is sometimes shortened to just You all or Who cooks for you? The Barred Owl's call is probably the first that many people recognize as being an owl's.

When a family group of Barred Owls get calling together, the result is a cacophony of hoots, wails, and whines. These noisy owls also shriek and scream. Barred Owls hoot during the day more than other owls, particularly on cloudy days.

NESTING BEHAVIOR

Barred Owls inhabit swamps and mixed forests, often favoring wet woods. They nest in natural cavities and snags, and they will readily nest in houses especially designed for them. They also take over abandoned squirrel, crow, and hawk nests.

Barred Owl *continued*

A BACKYARD OWL

In winter in the northern states, Barred Owls often turn up in yards where they may watch bird feeders for several days. However, they are more likely watching or listening for mice and voles drawn to the spilled seed around the feeder than the northern cardinals and blue jays dining on sunflower seeds at the feeder.

A winter that brings heavily crusted snow causes problems for Barred Owls, which are unable to punch through the crust to grab rodents tunneling beneath. Hunger can drive the owls to hunt along roads or scavenge road-killed animals. Many Barred Owls die from being struck by cars and they may become entangled in soccer goal nets, where they will perish unless rescued.

Barred Owls may wander in winter, sometimes turning up in cities to hunt rats, mice, squirrels, and pigeons. This one spent some time in Boston roosting on a large Christmas tree during the day. At dusk, it often dined on pigeon in full view of either horrified or fascinated commuters and holiday shoppers.

ON THE MENU

Barred Owls prey primarily on small mammals but also catch ones up to the size of rabbits. They hunt birds, insects, reptiles, and even fish and crayfish.

Flying squirrels

Screech owl

Red squirrels

Snakes

Songbirds

Worms

Grasshoppers

Fish

Crayfish

Bats

Chipmunks

Salamanders

Small frogs

Voles

Mice

Perched atop a mound of dead grass, a Barred Owl rests after capturing a long-tailed weasel.

Great Gray Owl

Strix nebulosa   OLD NAMES: Cinereous Owl

IDENTIFICATION

Wow! That's what you'll say when you see your first Great Gray Owl. It's North America's largest owl, with a huge head and up to a 5-foot wingspan and 30-inch-long body. Note the relatively small yellow-and-black eyes in the center of fine rings on the huge facial disks and the white "bow tie" just below the beak.

LENGTH: 23.5-33 INCHES

crow

WEIGHT: 1.7-3.2 POUNDS

WINGSPAN: 48.5-60 INCHES

Compared with other owls, Great Grays have relatively small eyes, which appear even smaller than they are because of their huge facial disks.

RANGE AND HABITAT

Great Gray Owls live in boreal forests in Canada, Alaska, and a few northern states: Montana, Minnesota, Oregon, Washington, and Wyoming. On rare years, Great Gray Owl irruptions from Canada disperse hundreds of owls southward.

Year-round

Winter Irruption

VOICE

Few people are fortunate enough to hear a Great Gray Owl. They're not usually heard away from the breeding area in boreal forest. The territorial call is a series of deep, low **hoots** that don't carry far through the woods.

Might Be Mistaken For

A Great Gray Owl may be mistaken for a Barred Owl (page 72), though the Barred Owl is much smaller. The best way to tell them apart is to notice eye color.

The Barred Owl's eyes appear black (dark brown in bright light when viewed through binoculars), while the Great Gray Owl's eyes are yellow with black pupils.

In the winter of 2004, thousands of Great Gray Owls moved south from Canada, appearing from New England to Montana. In Minnesota, some estimates pegged the statewide count at more than 5,000 birds.

A Great Gray Owl surveys its surroundings from its nest high above the ground.

A youngster that has left the nest but can't yet fly is called a brancher.

NESTING BEHAVIOR

During the nesting season, these huge owls are secretive and especially hard to spot. The vast boreal forests of Canada and Alaska make finding a nesting Great Gray Owl a long shot indeed. At the nest, the adults sometimes aggressively attack human intruders.

In the northern part of their breeding range, Great Gray Owls frequently use the old stick nests of hawks and crows. In the southern parts of the breeding range, Great Gray Owls often nest in tree snags rather than a stick nest.

Females lay an average of two or three eggs. Incubation lasts a month, and the babies leave the nest after about another month.

A BOLD CHARACTER

Perhaps more than any other owl (except maybe the Northern Saw-whet Owl), Great Gray Owls often show no fear of people and accept their presence. A visiting Great Gray may linger in one area for days or weeks if food is abundant.

In winters when one or two Great Gray Owls show up within easy driving distance of densely populated areas, large crowds of birders and photographers will flock to view this grand bird.

Right: Great Gray Owls often show little fear of people. This one thinks a bird-watcher makes a good landing spot!

A GREAT HUNTER

Great Gray Owls have legendary hearing. Their asymmetric ear openings, surrounded by huge facial disks (which are asymmetric as well) are very efficient at gathering sound.

Once during a windy snowstorm, I watched a Great Gray Owl stare intently at a spot in the snow some 90 feet away. Moments later, the owl launched at the spot and without hesitation plunged into a foot or more of snow, where it pulled a large meadow vole from its tunnel.

The owl couldn't have seen the vole under the deep snow; it heard it from 90 feet away, despite the interfering noise of high wind and the sound-muffling snow cover.

When a Great Gray Owl comes in for a landing feet-first, it leaves a different imprint than if it dove head down after a vole (below).

ON THE MENU

Great Gray Owls have relatively small feet and talons. They prey primarily on voles and other small animals.

Voles

Lemmings

Snowshoe hares

Red squirrels

Small frogs

Shrews

Long-eared Owl

Asio otus

IDENTIFICATION

This slim, medium-sized owl with long ear tufts and yellow-and-black eyes often roosts in dense trees. The streaked, strongly patterned belly is a good field mark as is a vertical dark stripe that runs through each eye.

LENGTH: 13-16 INCHES

crow

WEIGHT: 9-11 OUNCES

WINGSPAN: 36-42 INCHES

RANGE AND HABITAT

Although they range across the United States and Canada, Long-eared Owls are scarce in many places and easily overlooked because their roosts are well concealed. This uncommon owl is almost certainly undercounted on Christmas Bird Counts and breeding bird atlas projects.

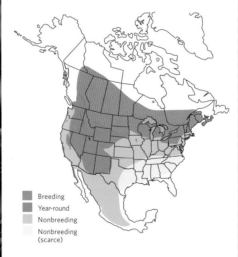

Breeding
Year-round
Nonbreeding
Nonbreeding (scarce)

VOICE

The Long-eared Owl calls at night with a low single hoot that might be repeated every few seconds. Be aware that Barred Owls also give single hoots, and many voice records of Long-eared Owls might in fact be Barred Owls. Use caution in identifying Long-eared Owls on voice alone.

Might Be Mistaken For

When perched, Long-eared Owls are easily confused with Great Horned Owls (page 50). Great Horned Owls show heavy barring on their flanks and belly. Long-eared Owls are streaked, not barred, on the belly.

In flight, Long-eared Owls strongly resemble Short-eared Owls, though the latter don't have the brown-orange face color of the Long-eared Owl.

LOOK CAREFULLY

Long-eared Owls can be frustratingly difficult to see. They sit in dense bushes and trees, their camouflage melting into the forest. In winter, they often roost in a group. If you find one Long-eared Owl, look carefully to see if others are roosting nearby. Also check to see if a Short-eared Owl (page 80) has joined the group.

In the eastern United States, large communal roosts of Long-eared Owls have become rare for reasons that aren't clear. In the West, communal roosts seem to be more common.

Top left: In Eastern Europe, huge communal roosts may contain 100 or more Long-eared Owls. North America can't claim such big roosts. How many can you spot in this photo?

BEHAVIOR

Long-eared Owls reuse the stick nests of crows, magpies, ravens, and various raptors. Studies show that they usually have a new mate each year.

While they roost in dense trees by day, Long-eared Owls hunt over fields, grasslands, farms, and marshes by night, which is where the similar Short-eared Owl also hunts.

Above: These chicks barely fit under their mother's wings but still need her protection.

Left: When stressed, a Long-eared Owl goes into a concealment posture: it pulls in its feathers, raises its ear tufts, and makes itself very skinny, trying to resemble a tree branch. If you see a Long-eared Owl "going skinny" like that, give the owl a lot more space. Even better, leave the area so the owl can nap undisturbed.

ON THE MENU

Long-eared Owls primarily hunt rodents, though they will sometimes eat snakes, lizards, bats, and songbirds.

Snakes

Pocket gophers

Moles

Songbirds

Mice

Shrews

Cottontail rabbits

Voles

Rats

Bats

Red squirrels

Lizards

Short-eared Owl

Asio flammeus   OLD NAMES: Bog Owl, Marsh Owl

IDENTIFICATION

A slender, medium-sized owl, the Short-eared Owl has light yellowish coloring with a streaked belly. Black triangular eye patches contrast with its yellow eyes and make the owl look like it's wearing eye shadow. The tiny ear tufts are rarely visible on the round head. In flight, look for the pale, buffy wing patches on the topside of the primary feathers.

LENGTH: 13-17 INCHES

crow

WEIGHT: 0.45-1.2 POUNDS

WINGSPAN: 38-44 INCHES

RANGE AND HABITAT

The Short-eared Owl breeds across northern states in the West and most of Canada, including the Arctic tundra, though it is rare in many areas. It often inhabits the same places as northern harriers (a type of hawk).

These owls winter widely across the eastern United States, but they are uncommon and have mostly disappeared as nesters. Sadly, they seem to be declining over much of North America.

Breeding
Year-round
Nonbreeding

VOICE

Often quiet except during nesting season, the male sings a series of **poo-poo-poo** notes in rapid succession for about two seconds. The alarm call is a series of hoarse **chiff-chiff-chiff-chiff** notes.

In competitive hunting situations around northern harriers and other Short-eared Owls, the Short-eared Owl will bark a sharp **yee-uck** call or give a wheezy complaining **screee**.

IN FLIGHT

The flight of the Short-eared Owl is buoyant and mothlike as it hunts over marshes, grasslands, and sand plains. More than any other owl, Short-eared Owls are usually first spotted in flight as they hunt.

The courtship flight of a male Short-eared Owl involves a spectacular wing clapping that's surprisingly sharp and loud. The claps come on the downbeat and usually involve three or four rapid claps that cause the bird to lose altitude. All this is done for the benefit of a female, who's perched nearby evaluating the show.

Above: A Short-eared Owl mother broods two chicks at her ground nest. The pantry (upper left) is stocked with voles, thanks to her attentive mate who has cached the food within easy reach.

NESTING BEHAVIOR

Short-eared Owls nest on the ground or in low bushes and trees, where they are vulnerable to predators like raccoons, skunks, coyotes, foxes, and roaming pet cats and dogs. Short-eared Owls sometimes roost in groups and occasionally will roost in trees with Long-eared Owls (page 78).

Because they hunt by day as well as night, Short-eared Owls are often harassed by gulls and crows.

Might Be Mistaken For

When viewed in flight at a distance in low light, Short-eared Owls strongly resemble Long-eared Owls (page 78). Both owls sometimes hunt the same fields or wet meadows. When perched, the ear tufts on a Short-eared Owl aren't usually visible, whereas the ear tufts on a Long-eared Owl usually are.

Don't rely on the presence or "lack" of ear tufts to separate these owls. Long-eared Owls have an orange-brown facial disk color, while Short-eared Owls lack the orange color on the face.

ON THE MENU

Short-eared Owls prey mostly on mice and voles, though some will hunt various birds and rabbits.

Mice

Cottontail rabbits

Voles

Shorebirds

Gulls

Pocket gophers

Rats

Songbirds

Bats

Lemmings

Boreal Owl

Aegolius funereus　　OLD NAMES: Richardson's Owl, American Sparrow Owl

IDENTIFICATION

The smallish, blocky, big-headed Boreal Owl has a finely spotted forehead and larger spotting on its chest and belly. The beak is greenish or bone colored, not black. Dark smudges appear on the lower outer facial disks.

LENGTH: 8.25-11 INCHES

crow

WEIGHT: 3-7.6 OUNCES

WINGSPAN: 19-24.5 INCHES

Boreal Owls are common, but they are rarely seen since the boreal forest is vast and observers are few.

RANGE AND HABITAT

The Boreal Owl favors old-growth spruce-fir-aspen forest in Alaska and across Canada. As the name suggests, this is an owl of the northern forests (the word *boreal* means "northern").

These owls also breed in the high peaks of the Rockies as far south as New Mexico. A juvenile found in the summer of 2001 in New Hampshire's White Mountains suggests that Boreal Owls may nest in northern New England more than is realized.

Year-round

VOICE

The song of the male Boreal Owl is a rapid trill of whistled po-po-po-po notes gaining volume and perhaps pitch toward the end, lasting two or three seconds. This call carries well in the forest and can be heard from quite a distance.

Might Be Mistaken For

See the discussion under Northern Saw-whet Owl (page 84).

Juvenile Boreal Owls look like they have been dipped in milk chocolate.

This small owl's fortunes are closely linked to vole populations.

LOOKING FOR FOOD

Boreal Owls don't usually migrate but they will expand their hunting range when necessary, a behavior called **irruptive migration**. Some rodent species, like voles, go through phases when their population grows when food is plentiful and then crashes when the food supply decreases. This means that the predators who depend on them have to look elsewhere for food.

When a Boreal Owls turns up in an urban setting such as Central Park in New York City, scores of birders turn out to see it. One Boreal Owl spent several days roosting in a yew tree on Commonwealth Avenue in Boston, Massachusetts, hunting rats and mice at night. Another roosted in a tree by a middle school in Newton, Massachusetts, much to the excitement of the students.

NESTING BEHAVIOR

Boreal Owls form new pairs each breeding season. They nest in cavities in aspen and poplar trees but hunt and roost in spruce-fir forest. The female lays on average three to five eggs and rarely uses the same nest cavity for two consecutive years. Chicks fledge in four to five weeks.

ON THE MENU

Boreal Owls mostly eats voles, but when voles are scarce, they also take mice, shrews, flying squirrels, young snowshoe hares, and small songbirds. Boreal Owls often cache food, tucking mice and voles into crevices and nooks of spruce and fir trees.

In winter, a Boreal Owl may thaw a frozen cached vole by holding the rodent in its foot up against its belly.

Flying squirrels · Crickets · Shrews · Beetles · Moths · Grasshoppers · Robins · Mice · Snowshoe hares · Bats · Sparrows · Pocket gopher · Squirrels · Chipmunks · Voles · Wrens

Northern Saw-whet Owl

Aegolius acadicus   OLD NAMES: Acadian Owl, Saw-Filer

IDENTIFICATION

The Northern Saw-whet Owl has yellow-and-black eyes, a black beak, and a rounded head (no ear tufts). Feathers are mottled brown and white, with a white V over the beak. With its elfin size and shape, this is the smallest owl in the East. In the West only the Elf Owl and the Flammulated Owl are smaller.

LENGTH: 7-8.5 INCHES

crow

WEIGHT: 2.5-4.5 OUNCES

WINGSPAN: 17-20 INCHES

RANGE AND HABITAT

Northern Saw-whet Owls breed in southeastern Alaska through the southern half of Canada into northern half of the eastern United States, and throughout the West, as well along the Appalachian chain into North Carolina and Tennessee. They prefer mixed forests, frequently near water.

They are migratory, though their wintering areas in the southeastern United States are poorly understood. Bird banders in the United States (see page 106) regularly handle large numbers of migrating Northern Saw-whet Owls, so the species must be fairly common in forests of the North.

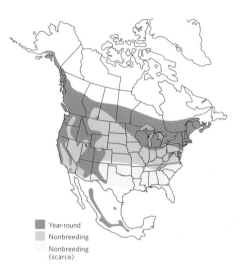

Year-round
Nonbreeding
Nonbreeding (scarce)

VOICE

The male's song is a rapid series of **whistled toots** that from a distance can sound like the backup alert on a truck. These owls also **bark** and **screech**.

Might Be Mistaken For

Northern Saw-whet Owls are similar to Boreal Owls (page 82), though smaller. One of the best field marks is on the forehead: Northern Saw-whet Owls have finely streaked foreheads, while Boreal Owls have finely spotted foreheads. Saw-whets have black beaks, while Boreals have greenish or bone-colored beaks.

BEHAVIOR

Northern Saw-whet Owls are difficult to find, as they are masters at hiding, usually roosting in thick evergreens or bushes. They nest in tree cavities made by woodpeckers and they readily use nest boxes.

They lay four to seven eggs and may raise two broods a year. The incubation period averages 28 days. The owlets fledge in about 30 days.

HUNTING METHODS

Saw-whets are nocturnal hunters, and they often use a perch-and-pounce hunting technique. They may cache prey for later eating. If you find a mouse or vole carcass (whole or partial) tucked into a nook in a spruce tree, suspect that a Northern Saw-whet Owl left it there.

Northern Saw-whet Owls may starve when deep snow topped by an icy crust makes capturing rodents difficult. In severe winters, homeowners occasionally find a weakened owl perched in a garage or under a porch roof or in shrubbery next to the house. The owl should be gently captured and brought to a licensed wildlife rehabilitator for evaluation.

Right: If you are lucky enough to stumble upon one, a Northern Saw-whet Owl will likely sit tight and not fly away from the protective cover of its perch.

ON THE MENU

Northern Saw-whet Owls eat insects, spiders, rodents, shrews, moles, and small birds. They will cache food, particularly in winter.

I have observed captive Northern Saw-whet Owls thaw frozen mice by holding them in their feet, pressed up against their body.

Spiders
Moles
Shrews
Crickets
Beetles
Small birds
Mice

THE HARDEST PART OF IDENTIFYING AN OWL IS FINDING IT. Most birds are **diurnal** (active during the day) and may be quite colorful or easy to see. However, finding an owl presents a bigger challenge. Most owls are **nocturnal** (more active at night), when your vision is at its weakest. With its quiet flight, you won't hear it as it flies over your head in the darkness. But with preparation and persistence, you will find owls!

OWLS ARE HARD TO SPOT

There's no denying that owls are tougher to find than most other birds. But that makes it all the sweeter when you finally spot one. Even experienced bird-watchers have trouble finding owls. Here are some tips on how to locate owls in the wild.

The best time to see an owl? Daytime. The best time to hear an owl? Nighttime.

A tool that will help you in your owl quest is a good pair of binoculars. When you look through binoculars, distant things are enlarged or magnified. Binoculars make birds appear closer, and you'll better see the details of the bird.

One of the best ways to see an owl is to hang out with bird-watchers who know how and where to find owls. Go on an "owl prowl" or some other organized bird walk led by experienced birders. Nature centers, Audubon groups, museums, and birding clubs are great places to find organized owl prowls.

When it comes to learning about owls or any other birds, it's great to spend time with people who know more than you. Most birders love to share their knowledge and are quick to help a newcomer learn the ropes of birding and owl finding. As a young person, you probably have sharper eyesight and better hearing than many adult birders, so you have much to offer them, too.

ABOVE: Finding an owl in the wild is exciting, but if you are having trouble spotting one, visit a zoo or science center to see owls in captivity. This will help you get a good idea of what you're looking for. (See page 117 for a list of places that have owls on display or offer owl programs.)

OPPOSITE: An Eastern Screech-Owl keeps watch from its perch in a cavity in a great oak tree.

LOOK AND LOOK AGAIN

Owls don't often call during the day. Many are crepuscular, which means that they become more active or vocal at twilight — the time just after sunset or just before sunrise. At night, an owl's call will alert you to its presence in the vicinity. But *seeing* one at night is another matter.

Owls have great camouflage and tend to sit in spots where they "disappear" for hours during daylight. Some are wary of people, fleeing at the distant appearance of a person. Some are small, making it even tougher to spot them.

By now you might be getting discouraged. You might be thinking, "I'll never find an owl." So let's get down to the business of finding an owl so you won't end up like the fifth grader who complained, "I'm outside a lot and I never see them!"

Often you'll hear owls rather than see them. If you're lucky, you'll see an owl while it is hooting. Notice how this Great Horned Owl's throat feathers ruffle up when it calls.

Snowy Owls can be sneaky. I've often seen them peeking at me from behind a snowdrift on the winter beach, like this one, or behind a mound of plants on the Arctic's summer tundra. All you might see is the very top of its white head and a hint of two lemon-pie eyes studying you.

GO OUTSIDE

You can learn a lot about owls from books, but spending time outdoors is an even better way to learn about owls and their habits. Owls aren't found everywhere — you need to know where to look. Like all animals, owls need to live in places that offer them shelter, food, and a safe place to raise their families. Another word for those places is **habitat**. If you know what kind of habitat different owls live in, you are more likely to spot them.

For example, 16 of the 19 species of owls in this book spend a lot of time in trees. Urban owls who nest in trees frequently live in parks, cemeteries, school and museum campuses, wildlife sanctuaries and refuges, and arboretums. Other places to look are capped landfills, airports, floodplains, and the marshes and woods around reservoirs. Paved treeless parking lots? Not so much.

A good way to learn where to find owls in your neighborhood is to track other people's bird sightings through eBird (ebird.org). This website, developed by Cornell University's Lab of Ornithology, helps birders share their sightings with others.

While responsible birders won't post a location of nesting owls (in order to protect the chicks and nervous parents from too many curious onlookers), many will report owl locations outside the nesting season. A few hours spent scanning other birders' checklists can help you find owls in your area.

If you have trees in your neighborhood, there's a good chance you have owls living nearby, like this Eastern Screech-Owl perched by a busy road.

LEARNING BY LISTENING

Because so much of owl searching is done by listening, it's good practice to listen to owl calls on the Internet. Some websites let you download calls to your phone, iPod, or computer so you can replay them as many times as you want. This will help you commit the calls to memory. If you have a smartphone, you can download birding apps that have owl calls. Birding apps have replaced hard-copy field guides for many birders.

BRING YOUR BINOCULARS

Searching for and studying owls is more fun when you can see them up close, even from a distance. A decent pair of binoculars costs about $125 (cheaper ones aren't worth the money). A good magnification measurement for most people is 7×35 mm or 8×40 mm. Choose a pair with a single focus knob instead of individual ones for each lens.

WHO'S WATCHING "HOO"?

With owls, the question becomes "Who's watching *you*?" Owls prefer watching to being watched. They observe their surroundings, always paying attention to what or who is near them. By the time you've spotted an owl, the owl has surely seen you first and has been studying you, gauging your intent.

Can you spot all the owls hiding here?

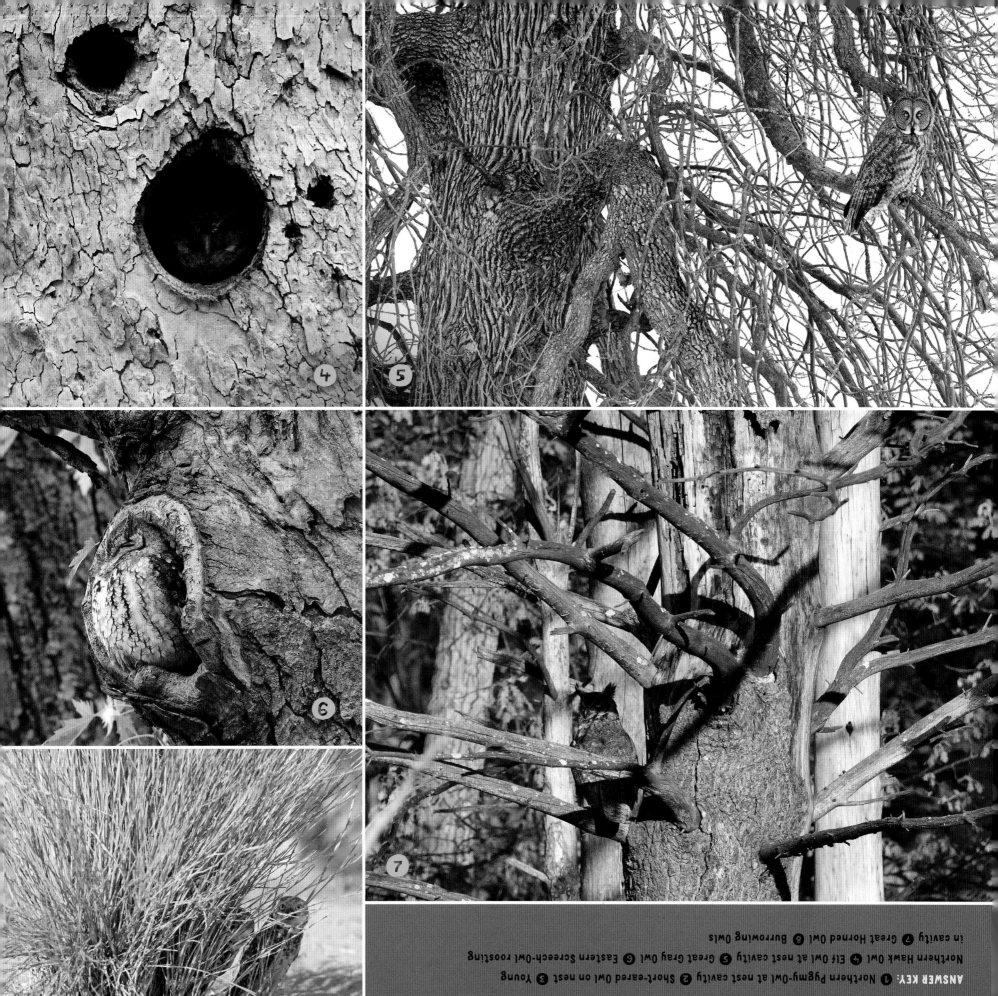

ANSWER KEY: ① Northern Pygmy-Owl at nest cavity ② Short-eared Owl on nest ③ Young Northern Hawk Owl ④ Elf Owl at nest cavity ⑤ Great Gray Owl ⑥ Eastern Screech-Owl roosting in cavity ⑦ Great Horned Owl ⑧ Burrowing Owls

POOP AND PELLETS

While a calling owl tells you it's nearby, other clues are important, too. One useful sign that shows where owls hang out is bird poop, or whitewash. All birds poop, but because owls often roost in the same place for many days, whitewash can pile up on the ground under the tree or cliff.

Whitewash also can build up on branches or run down the trunks of trees. Fresh whitewash is watery, while dried whitewash hardens and looks like chalky white paint. Sometimes tree sap looks like whitewash. Pine, fir, spruce, and hemlock trees have sap resembling owl whitewash. Don't be fooled!

Whitewash is a thick liquid that contains both urine and feces.

WHAT ARE PELLETS?

Another great clue for locating owls is owl pellets, which look like oval or oblong blobs of fur. They are regurgitated by the owl — that means that the pellet comes out of the owl's mouth and not out of its rear end, where whitewash is excreted. Old pellets that have weathered often look like balls of bones without much fur visible.

Some people call owl pellets "owl puke" or "owl vomit," but those names are not accurate. When people throw up, it's a sign they are sick. Owls regurgitate pellets daily as part of their normal body functions.

Pellets contain all the undigested remains of whatever animal the owl ate. In a pellet you'll find fur, skulls, bones, beaks, feathers, fish scales, or insect parts.

Animal feces (poop) from a raccoon or fox can look like owl pellets, so don't use your bare hands to pick up anything you find. One clue that helps separate feces from pellets is that pellets hardly ever contain seeds, berries, or other plant matter. That's because owls are **carnivores**; they eat meat rather than vegetables, seeds, or fruit.

Bottom right: Lots of whitewash and piles of pellets mark a roosting site for Boreal Owls.

Pellet regurgitation is not a sign of sickness; on the contrary, it is the habit of a healthy owl!

pellet

How an Owl Pellet Is Formed

esophagus

glandular stomach

muscular stomach

intestines

vent

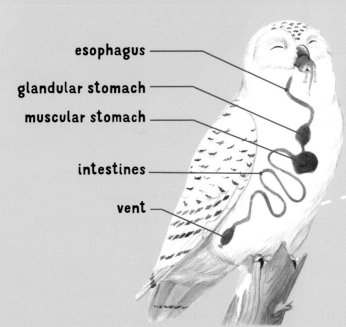

1 Prey that is swallowed whole is positioned properly before passing into the esophagus.

2 In the glandular stomach, enzymes break down the food and begin to extract nutrients.

One time I found a Long-eared Owl pellet that contained kernels of corn! The owl had eaten a dove or pigeon that had eaten corn. The corn passed through the owl undigested and ended up in the pellet.

3 The muscular stomach grinds and presses the bones and hair into a pellet.

4 Digestible material passes through the intestines, which absorb nutrients.

5 After 8 to 10 hours, the pellet is disgorged. Whitewash is expelled through the vent.

TAKING APART A PELLET

Today is owl pellet day at Eliot Elementary School in Eliot, Maine. Devan Weber's third grade class has been looking forward to this day for weeks.

"Make sure everyone has two toothpicks, a paper cup, tweezers, and a paper towel," says Mrs. Weber. The students will share handheld magnifiers. At their desks, each student is given a dark, grayish Barn Owl pellet.

"They look like little burritos," says Mrs. Weber, inspecting the pellets, which come wrapped in aluminum foil. The students talk excitedly as they unwrap their pellets and begin to pick them apart.

"I should give this [pellet] to my mom on Mother's Day," says Michael, grinning.

"Eeww, gross!" responds the girl next to him.

"Oh, this is disgusting," says Leila. "It smells like . . . I can't even explain."

"Dude, look at that!" exclaims Martin to the boy next to him. "My skull has a hole through it," he says, referring to a rodent's skull and not his own head.

"I found a jawbone," exclaims Maria.

"I found a skull with a nose bone," announces Tyrone.

"Look, it's a vertebra from a mole," says Jason, holding a tiny bone.

"Oh, yeah!" says Kendal, admiring it through a magnifying glass.

Mrs. Weber makes the rounds, watching her students extract bones and skulls, advising and encouraging them. "Keep digging," she says as she notices some students just staring into piles of

Snowy Owl pellet on the beach

Long-eared Owl pellet

Jawbones from a Spotted Owl pellet

Long-eared Owl pellets with bird skull

Snowy Owl pellets

Great Horned Owl pellet on forest floor

fur. "Some of the bones are as small as a period."

She pauses to look at a bone. "That is the tiniest pelvis I've ever seen," says Mrs. Weber. The girl who found it looks pleased and goes back to picking through her pellet.

By lunch, the students have extracted all the bones from their pellets, leaving behind piles of fur. When they return to class, the kids match the bones to a chart that identifies different types. After they sort all the bones, the students begin to match them to a diagram of a rodent's skeleton and glue them in place.

Jason needs leg bones to fill out his rodent skeleton diagram. Next to Jason, Julia has amassed an impressive number of little bones, heaped on her bone sorting chart. Jason looks over at her pile of bones. "Julia, see these bones?" asks Jason, pointing. "Can I have them? I need legs." Julia gives him a few leg bones. Her pellet contained bones from more than one rodent.

By the end of the school day, some of the kids are still gluing. Their glued skeleton diagrams will dry overnight. Lots of kids have extra bones left over. "You can take the extra ones home," Mrs. Weber announces to the class. "Choose a snack-sized plastic bag — you don't need a gallon-sized bag for mouse bones!"

"This is my favorite activity of all time," says Jason. "I wish I could do this every day."

Dissecting pellets takes patience and careful handling. Most of the bones you find are pretty small.

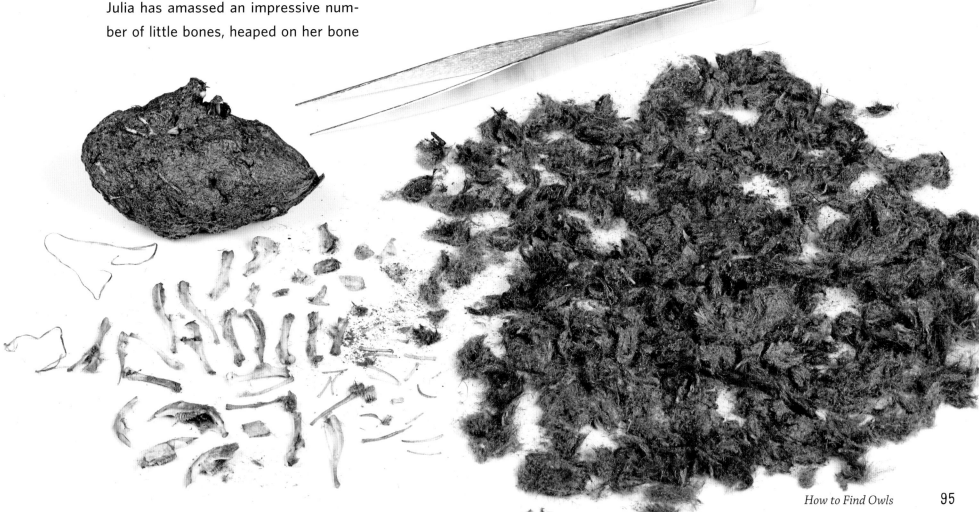

Following the Clues

Say you find a lot of whitewash and pellets on the ground underneath a pine tree. Take several steps back from the tree and look up into the branches. Binoculars will greatly help you search the upper parts of the tree.

Carefully study each branch. Examine where the branches join the trunk of the tree. Let your eyes follow the branches out to where the pine needles are dense.

Take your time searching. You'll see more details if you don't hurry. If there's an owl up there, you might only see a small part of its body or head. If you are lucky, you will see the owl's eyes squinting down at you.

The pile of whitewash beneath this tree was a good sign that Boreal Owls roosted there. Notice the owl watcher using binoculars to study the owl from a distance.

How to Find Owls

OWL ETIQUETTE

Seeing an owl is a privilege. The number one thing to remember when you are around an owl is that it's a wild animal. You should practice certain owl manners to make the owl comfortable and keep yourself safe.

The main rule when you're looking for wildlife is to use a quiet voice. Owls and other animals react to loud noises. Even a normal conversation sounds loud to them, so if you have to talk, do so in a whisper.

Owls read your body language before you even realize they are watching. If you move slowly and quietly, and don't stare directly at an owl for too long, it might accept your presence. But if you run, talk loudly, or flail your arms excitedly, the owl may flee the commotion.

DON'T GO TOO CLOSE

An owl rarely leaves the security of its hidden roost (that would be dangerous), but if you move too close and its eyes pop wide open, it's a sign that you should back up and give the owl its space.

While owls rarely attack people, there are times when you should leave owls alone. Avoid getting close to owl nests or owlets that have just left the nest, day or night. Owls that are defending their babies may aggressively fly at nearby people. It's rare, but owls

Long-eared Owl

have struck people in the head or face with their talons.

Even small screech owls can be defensive when they are raising babies. Great Horned Owls, Great Gray Owls, Barred Owls, and Snowy Owls have all been known to strike people near the nest. You are particularly at risk if an owl attacks at night, since you won't see or hear it coming.

KEEP THEIR SECRETS

Owls sleeping on a roost are easily disturbed by loud noises, dogs, or lots of people talking and moving about. It's okay to be vague about the location of owls you find, especially as you learn how to practice good owl manners and which people you can trust to approach owls with respect and caution. The welfare of the owl should always come first.

TALKING TO OWLS

Using recorded owl calls or hooting by mouth can be useful for attracting owls, but only if you do it in a responsible way. Overuse of recorded calls will stress out owls, and you don't want to do that!

Birders on a Christmas Bird Count, owl researchers taking a census, and birders building their life lists may need to imitate owl calls to get a response. But imitating an owl's call, whether by mouth or audio playback, comes with responsibilities and rules. It's important that owls don't suffer from our careless behavior.

Follow these simple rules to ensure the safety and well-being of the owls you long to hear and see.

RULE 1

Follow the season. Don't use recorded calls in the breeding and nesting season, which for most owls runs from late winter to midsummer. Hearing calls may make owls think there's an intruder in their territory. A male owl might fly in to investigate, which wastes energy and is stressful, especially in winter.

RULE 2

Know the law. It's illegal to use playback for any birds, not just owls, in national wildlife refuges, national parks, and most wildlife sanctuaries. You should also avoid using audio playback in places visited by lots of birders, since some of them may already be using playback in that area. You wouldn't want to overload these birds with stressful intruder calls.

RULE 3

Don't overdo it. Playing a recorded call night after night in the same spot (say your backyard) might cause an owl to abandon its territory. You could end up driving away the very owl you're trying to see. So mix up the locations where you try using audio playback. Don't use playback calls in the same spot more than once a year.

RULE 4

Take your time. Play an owl call once or twice and then stop. Wait for three or four minutes to see if you get a response. Sometimes, an owl will fly from some distance to check out your intruder call. The incoming owl may stay silent and observe you from overhead trees. Watch for silent passing shadows that show you an owl has arrived.

RULE 5

Keep it quiet. Use medium volume for your call playback. It's a rookie mistake to play a call too frequently or too loudly.

If you're patient (and lucky!), an owl may answer your call, like this Great Horned is doing.

OWL-FRIENDLY ENVIRONMENT

A perfectly manicured lawn isn't a good place for animals to find food. Having lots of different plants in your yard makes a more welcoming habitat for the insects and small animals that more owls hunt for. Here are a few things you can do to attract owls to your backyard.

PROVIDE NESTING SITES. Many owls like to nest in tree cavities like this one, but you can put up a nest box instead (see pages 100–101).

PUT UP A BIRD FEEDER. Owls don't eat birdseed, but they know that other birds do and they keep an eye on neighborhood feeders. At night, small mammals come looking for spilled seed, providing more menu options for a hungry owl.

GO A LITTLE WILD. Leave a section of yard unmoved for most of the year. Letting the plants grow tall and the flowers ripen into seeds will attract small rodents and birds for owls to hunt.

PROVIDE WATER. A place to drink attracts animals of all kinds. Make a pool a few inches deep with sloped sides or flat stepping stones in it for easy access. Change the water frequently to keep it clean and discourage mosquitos from laying eggs.

BUILD A BRUSH PILE. A mound of small branches and clippings from bushes offers shelter for squirrels, chipmunks, mice, voles, and songbirds.

BUILD AN OWL HOUSE

How cool would it be if you didn't always have to search for owls in the woods, but instead could stay at home and have the owls came to you? Yeah, pretty cool.

The best way to attract owls to your neighborhood or yard is to offer them housing. A birdhouse for owls is your best bet for attracting owls that use tree cavities to nest. If your neighborhood doesn't have many big, old trees, there might be a shortage of good tree cavities in your area for owls to use for nesting. Putting up a couple of owl-sized birdhouses can help relieve that housing shortage.

Building an owl birdhouse is fairly easy and not very expensive. You need just six pieces of rough-cut pine to make an owl house. Cutting the boards to size requires use of sharp tools, so have an adult familiar with woodworking help you. An alternate option is to attend a birdhouse-building seminar or class to get help.

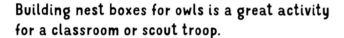

Building nest boxes for owls is a great activity for a classroom or scout troop.

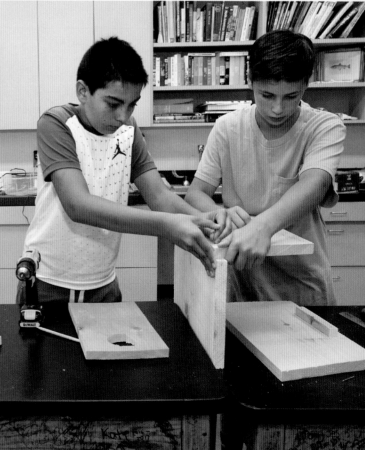

OWL HOUSES

Many smaller owls are cavity nesters. Putting up an owl nest box may attract one to your neighborhood. Building an owl birdhouse is fairly easy and not very expensive.

Visit www.storey.com/owl-nest-box/ to find plans for building a nesting box for these owls:

 Eastern Screech-Owl

 Western Screech-Owl

 Northern Saw-whet Owl

 **Whiskered Screech-Owl**

Find plans for building nest boxes for these owls at the Cornell Lab of Ornithology (nestwatch.org/learn/all-about-birdhouses).

 Elf Owl

 Boreal Owl

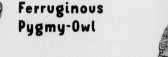 **Ferruginous Pygmy-Owl**

 Barred Owl

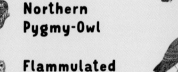 **Northern Pygmy-Owl**

 Barn Owl

Flammulated Owl

Many North American owls are cavity nesters, but a few are not. Don't expect these owls to use a birdhouse: Burrowing Owl, Great Gray Owl, Great Horned Owl, Long-eared Owl, Short-eared Owl, Northern Hawk Owl, and Snowy Owl.

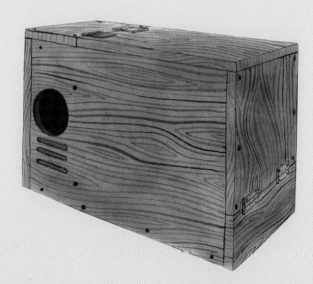

Before you build a nest box, like this one for a Barn Owl family, make sure you can place it in an appropriate spot, paying attention to the instructions for how high to hang it and what direction the opening should face. If you are lucky enough to attract a nesting pair, observe them from a distance without disturbing them. You don't want them to move away!

Barred Owl

Boreal Owl

Eastern Screech-Owl

Northern Saw-whet Owl

Barn Owl

Working with OWLS

MOST PEOPLE ARE AT LEAST INTERESTED IN OWLS, IF NOT FASCINATED BY THEM. But some people, like my wife, Marcia, and me, just can't get enough of their favorite raptors, so they find a way to make owls part of their everyday lives. Meet a few of those lucky people here, from raptor rehabilitators to wildlife researchers to an artist who says drawing owls is one of her favorite things to do.

OWLS IN THE CLASSROOM

MARCIA WILSON
Eyes On Owls
New Hampshire, USA

Marcia Wilson stands in a gym in an elementary school full of chattering, squirming third graders. Behind her are six wood carrying boxes with shiny brass hinges. Looking over the room, Marcia takes a deep breath and lets loose with a booming "Hoo-hoo-oo-oo, hoo, hoo," her voice quivering over the second set of notes. She has the kids' attention now. She hoots again.

"That's the call of an owl. Maybe you've heard it at night. Do you know what kind of owl is it?"

Hands shoot up. "Is it a hoot owl?" guesses a boy.

"Well, hoot owl is kind of a general name. I want to know what species, or kind, of owl it is."

The students float a few more guesses before a girl at the back of the class quietly states, "It's a Great Horned Owl."

"Yes! Very good," praises Marcia. She then asks the students why they think she's laid down a long walkway mat on the gym floor.

"In case the owls poop?" asks a grinning boy.

"It's not *in case* they poop, but *when* they poop. Owls poop just before they fly, to lighten the load." she explains. "But we call it whitewash, which is more polite."

The owls perched on Marcia's gloved hand sometimes try to fly off, but she keeps a tight grip on two leather straps called jesses, which go around each leg of the owl and are attached to a leash. An owl may poop and flap, but he can't leave Marcia's hand unless she releases the jesses.

Students often ask if the owls mind being kept up during the day for the programs. The answer is that they come out to "work" for just 10 or 15 minutes at a time and spend most of their day snoozing in their cozy dark carrying boxes.

Marcia brings out an Eastern Screech-Owl and whistles its call. She asks for a volunteer to come up and imitate the call. Hooting lessons and learning to identify an owl by its voice are a key part of the program, since wild owls are mostly nocturnal and many kids will hear an owl but not see it.

Marcia brings out a gray morph Eastern Screech-Owl with one eye missing. The kids quickly notice and ask about it. She explains that the owl was hit by a car. Someone brought it to a wildlife hospital, and the doctor had to remove the damaged eye. She goes on to highlight the field marks of the Eastern Screech-Owl: small size, yellow-and-black eyes, and ear tufts atop the head.

The kids learn that different owls hunt different prey at different times of the day. They add some new words to their vocabularies: diurnal (active during the day), nocturnal (active at night), and crepuscular (active at dusk).

Marcia discusses silent flight, bird's weights, rotating heads, fixed eyeballs, carnivorous diets, eggs and hatching, courtship, gripping pressure of owls' feet, talons, feather structure, and more, illustrating each topic with one of the owls.

OWLS ARE NOT PETS

If you think you'd like to have an owl as a pet, think again. In Canada, the United States, and many other countries, wild birds can't be kept in captivity. The owls you see in zoos and science centers are either permanently injured and can't be released back to the wild, or they were hatched in a zoo and raised by people.

Zoos, science centers, and educators in the United States must have permits from the U.S. Fish and Wildlife Service and their state wildlife agency in order to use these owls as educational birds.

OWL ARTIST, AUTHOR & TEACHER

CLARE WALKER LESLIE
Massachusetts and Vermont

Clare Walker Leslie sits in front of a large outdoor **aviary**, clasping a pencil and balancing a notebook on her lap. A Great Gray Owl perches 30 feet away, 15 feet up. The owl ignores Clare.

Clare ignores her paper, her hand moving as she stares at the owl, outlining its form in a rough pencil drawing. This is called blind contour drawing, and Clare does it to warm up, much like a runner stretching before a race.

Clare studied art history and music in college but soon realized that drawing and being out in nature was her true calling. With simple drawing tools and her trusty binoculars, she goes out in all kinds of weather, searching for the magic that comes with drawing birds.

An artist, teacher, and author of 12 books on studying and drawing nature, Clare encourages her students to picture a bird as having large circle for the body with a small circle on top for the head. Fine shapes and details are quickly added to this circle-on-circle framework. "Two circles. That's it. That's the essence of the bird, these two circles," says Clare.

Of course, it's not really that easy. "Drawing is extremely difficult, especially birds," she allows. "I've made thousands of bad drawings."

With that, Clare turns to a blank page and stares at the Great Gray Owl as if she's seeing it for the first time, deeply enjoying the company of the grandest of owls.

Clare always has a sketchbook with her so she can draw birds, animals, and plants — anything that is part of nature.

"Nature is in my blood," Clare says. "We naturalists can never be bored. There's too much for us to be curious about."

SAW-WHET OWL BANDER

KATHY SEYMOUR
Drumlin Farm Wildlife Sanctuary
Massachusetts Audubon Society
Lincoln, Massachusetts

If you want to band owls, you have to keep owl hours, which means you might run short on sleep. Kathy Seymour leaves her job around 4:30 P.M. to bolt down some supper before heading to the banding station at Massachusetts Audubon's Drumlin Farm Wildlife Sanctuary. She hopes to catch some migrating Northern Saw-whet Owls.

Most bird banders use fine black nylon nets called mist nets to capture birds without harming them. A properly set net has baglike folds that cradle the bird, making escape impossible. The nets are folded up when not in use.

On this Halloween night, conditions look promising for a good flight of Northern Saw-whet Owls. It's 44°F (7°C), with clear skies and a light wind. This is Kathy's 23rd night of banding this fall. Tonight, she hopes the group will net its 300th owl.

At the banding station, it sounds like a giant Northern Saw-whet Owl has taken over the dark forest. Its loud tooting call pulses repeatedly from nearby woods, played over a loudspeaker. The call attracts migrating owls into the area, where some are caught in the mist nets.

The banders check the nets every 45 minutes. Tonight, every net run brings in tiny owls. At 11:49 P.M., the 300th Northern Saw-whet Owl of the season is extracted. Everyone crowds around to ogle the star, a second-year female with a trace of body fat.

As the banders put away their nets for the night, the forest echoes with the squeals and toots of many Northern Saw-whet Owls. Kathy pauses to listen. "This is so cool," she says. "I wish I spoke their language so I could understand them better."

The goal is to collect data, but handling and observing this incredibly cute owl is the big reward.

1 Each captured owl is tucked into a soft cloth bag and carried back to the banding station.

2 The banders weigh the birds and score their body fat on a scale from 0 (none) to 7 (very excessive). Fat is important because it fuels flight muscles on long trips. This owl weighed 3.4 ounces, about the same as a small apple, which is average for a female.

3

The wing is measured from the wrist (the middle joint) to the tip.

6

Unbanded owls are fitted with an aluminum band that goes around its leg. Each band has a unique number so if it is caught again, the measurements can be compared.

4 Feather growth patterns in the wing show the owl's age. Old feathers are lighter brown and frayed. New feathers are darker with fresh edges. This owl is about three years old.

5

Newly grown wing feathers glow pink under a black light, showing that this owl hatched this season. Older feathers don't glow.

7 After she's measured and banded, the owl is brought outside. After a moment to regain her bearings and adjust to the night, she silently wings into the darkness.

OWL CARETAKER & EDUCATOR

SHEENA PATEL
Vermont Institute of Natural Science
Quechee, Vermont

When Sheena Patel attends a staff meeting, she often brings along Hartland, a Barred Owl. Hartland is an educational ambassador who stars (along with several other owls, hawks, and a vulture) in live raptor shows featured at the Vermont Institute for Natural Science (VINS). Sheena accustoms Hartland to groups of people by carrying her around on her gloved hand. To keep Hartland in touch with her forest roots, Sheena takes her on trail walks in the woods.

Sheena works as a wildlife rehabilitator at VINS. Once or twice a week, she fills in as presenter for the raptor shows. The raptors are trained by using food as a motivator, meaning the owls or hawks are rewarded with a tidbit of mouse or rat when they do something the trainer asks of them.

Sheena devotes a lot of time to Hartland, getting her used to different environments and teaching her to sit on a stand and enter a carrying case. She also tidies up Hartland's cage and prepares her meals.

Hartland, who was named after the town where she was found after falling from her nest, doesn't hoot loudly (and maybe can't). Instead, when Sheena is near, Hartland hoots very softly to her — so soft that it sounds like the hoots come from far away.

VINS treats all types of birds, including songbirds like cedar waxwings and Baltimore orioles, and wading birds like great blue herons. Birds arrive at VINS injured (often from car strikes), starving, or orphaned. The staff assesses new patients and comes up with a treatment plan. The care schedule can be grueling. Baby songbirds need to be fed every 30 to 60 minutes.

When the patients recover, sometimes they can be released back to the wild. "That's my favorite part, the releases," says Sheena.

> **"I'm a bird nerd,"
> Sheena cheerfully
> admits.**

Opposite: Sheena's tasks include preparing food, providing physical therapy for birds, giving regular checkups to patients, and cleaning cages. Sheena says she's scrubbed a lot of poop.

RAPTOR REHABILITATOR

MARIA COLBY
Wings of the Dawn
Henniker, New Hampshire

It's just after 8 P.M. when Maria Colby's cell phone rings. "There's a big owl sitting in the middle of the road," says the caller. "I think it's hurt. It doesn't seem like it can fly. What should I do?"

Maria clicks into her rescue instructions. "Approach the bird with a blanket or towel, throw it over the bird, and then wrap it up. Secure the bird in the trunk of your car, on the floor in the backseat, or in a cardboard box. Can you transport it to me?"

Another Barred Owl has been struck by a car. Of all the injured raptors Maria treats, Barred Owls are by far the most frequent patients. At night, the owls frequently fly across roads as they hunt or land to scavenge on road-killed squirrels, rabbits, raccoons, and beavers.

A small percentage of injured owls are rescued and brought to an animal hospital, a veterinarian, or a qualified wildlife rehabilitator like Maria Colby at Wings of the Dawn.

It takes flight and disappears back to its old life.

Maria tosses a rehabilitated owl into the night sky.

In a year, Maria treats more than 600 individual birds!

Conservation officer Shawn MacFadzen brings an injured Barred Owl for Maria to evaluate.

Some injured birds are brought in by concerned citizens. Sometimes a conservation officer from the New Hampshire Fish and Game Department will bring in a hawk, owl, or eagle. Often after the phone rings, Maria hustles out the door with heavy gloves, towels, and cardboard boxes to pick up a new patient.

Once Maria finds the injured raptor, she checks the bird carefully. Some injuries, like a broken wing, are obvious. Other injuries or diseases are harder to determine. Maria often brings the bird to a local veterinarian who takes x-rays and blood tests.

Some owls come in starving. Maria provides plenty of food, and once the owl reaches a good weight, she releases it back to the wild. Feeding time at Wings of the Dawn means thawing mice and rats from the chest freezer and making sure each patient gets enough food. Maria notes who is eating and who is not.

LEARNING ON THE WING

After treating and releasing many Barred Owls that had lost an eye, Maria wondered how well these birds survived after being returned to the wild. Many experts had opinions about this, but data was lacking, so Maria created an experiment. In 2016 she released four sight-impaired and five normally sighted Barred Owls back to the forest. All nine owls were fitted with radio transmitters, each with a different signal that could travel five miles or more.

Maria tracked each owl using a handheld antenna. She would cruise roads adjacent to the release site with her arm hanging out the car window, rotating the antenna to pick up signals. After picking up an owl's signal from two different locations, Maria used compass bearings to draw lines on a map to pinpoint where the owls were and keep track of their movements. After four months of tracking, Maria found that one-eyed owls seem to survive in the wild just fine.

These Great Horned Owls were released shortly after this picture was taken.

STUDENT OF OWLS

CARRIE WENDT
Humboldt State University
Arcata, California

In 1995, a couple of Napa Valley grape farmers put up nest boxes for Barn Owls in their vineyards. The farmers knew the owls would prey on rodents, which often chew bark off grapevines and gnaw roots. Pocket gophers in particular destroy irrigation lines and create large earth mounds that slow down workers. As word spread about how Barn Owls gobbled up voles and gophers, more vineyards installed Barn Owl nest boxes.

Twenty years later, Carrie Wendt, a graduate student at Humboldt State

University in California, needed a research topic for her master of science degree. Her thesis adviser suggested she study the grape farmers' perceptions of Barn Owls in their vineyards.

By this time, thousands of Barn Owl nest boxes dotted the area, and Carrie hoped her research would point out the best sites for them. She would study how habitat affected Barn Owl productivity. Did locating a nest box near grassland, woods, a tree, or buildings make a difference in the number of babies raised? Which types of boxes did Barn Owls use the most? Did nest box design and placement matter? Did Barn Owls fare better in organic vineyards or conventional vineyards using pesticides?

During the spring and summer of 2015 and 2016, Carrie spent most of her waking hours in the company of grapes and Barn Owls. Lots and lots of Barn Owls. She started out monitoring 297 nest boxes in 65 vineyards. She visited each box three times the first month, peeking into them with a camera on an extendable pole. The camera streamed video to her laptop computer or her phone so that she could see what the owls were doing. Sometimes she could hear the parents and baby owls hissing at the camera. Carrie found she

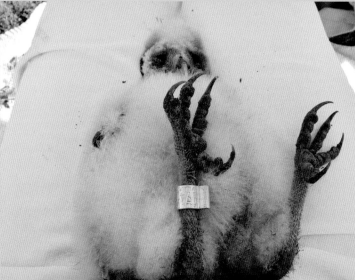

could check 85 boxes in a day, with each nest check taking about five minutes.

She worked by day to minimize disturbance to the owl families. At night, she camped in the vineyards, sleeping in the bed of her Toyota pickup truck. She drove 5,000 miles in a month. By the first of April, Carrie was monitoring only those nest boxes with owl families, numbering 94. During the second year of her study, Carrie watched 150 Barn Owl nest boxes, gathering more data.

She checked each box regularly until the owlets left around mid-July. She counted how many eggs hatched and how many chicks fledged. Some of her study owls were hit by cars, electrocuted on power lines, or preyed on by Great Horned Owls. She figures her Barn Owls were living for three years on average.

Carrie found that the habitat around the nest box predicted nest success. Owls were more plentiful in the southern part of the valley, where the vineyards are surrounded by open grasslands rather than chaparral scrub or oak forests that grow farther north. She was also able to educate farmers that poisoning rodents meant they were poisoning the owls. Carrie now works as a partner biologist, helping farmers, ranchers, and forest owners protect and improve their land for wildlife like bees, bats, and of course, Barn Owls.

"My job is fantastic," says Carrie.

Opposite: These babies hissed when removed from their nest boxes to be weighed and banded. Once outside, they rocked and bobbed or played dead as the strange two-legged creature handled them.

FERRUGINOUS PYGMY-OWL RESEARCHER

AARON FLESCH
University of Arizona
Tucson, Arizona

When Aaron Flesch first started studying Ferruginous Pygmy-Owls, "they were this mysterious species," he says. At the time, the owls were listed on the Federal Endangered Species List. To begin his work, Aaron looked for an area with lots of saguaros, where these little birds were known to nest. Then he set up a station at regular intervals where he could play a recorded call of the male Pygmy-Owl. If another male owl called back or flew in, Aaron knew he had a nesting territory.

Aaron learned that unpaired males would call all night, trying to attract a female, but paired males would soon fall silent after responding to the call. To locate nesting sites, he looks for pellets and poop near a saguaro cavity. He pokes a camera mounted on a pole into any promising cavities to see if it contains a female owl incubating eggs.

One of his surprising findings was that Elf Owls sometimes nest in a different cavity in the same saguaro as Ferruginous Pygmy-Owls. This happens especially in places where cavities are scarce. He also learned that pygmy owls won't nest within 400 to 500 yards of another pygmy owl pair.

Ferruginous Pygmy-Owls are mostly diurnal, but they are also active on nights around the full moon. By working on bright nights in April and May, Aaron can cram three days' worth of fieldwork into one 24-hour period.

In 2006, the owl was delisted as an endangered species, mostly for bureaucratic reasons. As Aaron gathers data about these fierce little desert owls that he is so good at finding, he thinks the owl may be relisted as endangered. His research may help make that decision.

When Aaron listens for calling owls, he cups his hands behind his ears to enhance his hearing. If it's not windy, Aaron can hear an owl calling up to 650 yards away.

FLAMMULATED OWL EXPERT

BRAD GRAEVS
Plumas Audubon Society
Quincy, California

It takes time and patience to find a Flammulated Owl. Brad Graevs, project manager of the Plumas Audubon Society, hikes through Plumas National Forest looking for Flammulated Owl nests in trees growing at an elevation of 6,000 feet or higher.

Brad lugs a long yellow fiberglass pole that telescopes up to 35 feet. At the tip of the pole sits a slim camera, which he neatly guides into small holes in selected trees. The camera transmits a real-time view of the hole to a video screen held by his assistant.

Brad also carries a passenger on his back — his two-year-old daughter, Calliope. They are exploring an area where trees have been cleared to help control forest fires. Fewer trees means fewer places for Flammulated Owls to nest, so Plumas Audubon has erected some 160 Flammulated Owl nest boxes, placed in both the cleared area and the nearby untouched forest. Brad's project is studying how well the small owls breed using the nest boxes and cavities in both areas.

Approaching a Douglas fir, Brad extends the camera pole, craning and straining his neck upward, guiding the camera into a cavity. "Does it go anywhere?" he asks.

His assistant peers down into a small video monitor. "No," she says, sounding slightly disappointed. They move on. The morning heats up as the researchers fan out to spot cavities and nest boxes in the forest. After a day of searching, the team has found no owls or any other cavity-nesting bird, which is somewhat surprising.

"We are detecting Flammulated Owls but we didn't find any nests. Zeroes are still data," says Brad, chuckling. After six years of studying the owls, he's already thinking about next summer's research. Somewhere back in the pines and firs, the Flamms wait, ready for another round of hide-and-seek.

Using a pole camera is like looking for fairies in tiny caves 35 feet up a tree.

Two-year-old Calliope proves that you can never be too young to be a birder!

GLOSSARY

aviary. A large building, cage or enclosure where birds are housed.

barring. Horizontal marks on a bird's chest, belly or undertail.

boreal. Of the North, as in boreal forest and boreal owl.

branching. Development stage when birds leave the nest before all their flight feathers are fully grown.

brood patch. Featherless patch of skin on a female bird's belly, where eggs are kept warm with direct contact of skin.

cache. To stockpile or hide something, like food, in a spot to be retrieved later.

carnivore. Meat eater.

clutch. A group of eggs laid by a female bird that are incubated all at the same time.

crepuscular. Active around dawn and dusk.

diurnal. Active during the day.

facial disks. Big saucers of fine feathers around the eyes.

field mark. Distinctive markings or behaviors that birders use to identify a bird.

habitat. Areas that offer shelter, food, and a safe place to raise families.

irruption, irruptive migration. When birds move unpredictably from year to year, usually in search of food in places far away from their nesting areas.

migratory. To nest in one place and move to a different location for the winter.

mobbing. Harassing or trying to drive one bird away from other birds' territory.

morph. Different color forms of birds. For example, Eastern Screech-Owls come in red, brown, and gray morphs.

nictitating membrane. A translucent third eyelid that acts as a movable shield that protects, cleans, and moistens the eye.

nocturnal. Active at night.

owlery. A place where owls are housed and cared for.

owlets. Tiny owl chicks.

permanent residents. Birds that live in the same area year-round and do not migrate.

raptors. Predator birds that catch their prey with their powerful feet.

rufous. Reddish.

talons. Claws made from the same material as human fingernails, but sharper, narrower and stronger.

taxonomists. Scientists who study the relationships of different animals.

thermals. Updrafts of air that raptors often use to provide lift.

whitewash. Liquid bird poop.

Great Gray Owl

PLACES TO SEE OWLS IN CAPTIVITY

Many, but not all, of the listed raptor centers have owls on display. Some centers offer live owl programs off-site at public venues. Call ahead to check program schedules or arrange a tour. The zoos and museums listed have owls on display.

UNITED STATES

Alabama
Alabama Wildlife Center
Pelham

Southeastern Raptor Center
Auburn

Alaska
Alaska Raptor Center
Sitka

Alaska Wildlife Conservation Center
Girdwood

Alaska Zoo
Anchorage

Arizona
Arizona-Sonora Desert Museum
Tucson

Arkansas
Raptor Rehab of Central Arkansas
El Paso

California
California Living Museum
Bakersfield

California Raptor Center
Davis

Los Angeles Zoo and Botanical Gardens
Los Angeles

San Diego Zoo
San Diego

San Francisco Zoo
San Francisco

Colorado
Nature and Wildlife Discovery Center
Pueblo

Rocky Mountain Raptor Program
Fort Collins

Connecticut
Audubon Sharon
Sharon

Connecticut's Beardsley Zoo
Bridgeport

Denison Pequotsepos Nature Center
Mystic

Delaware
Brandywine Zoo
Wilmington

Florida
Audubon Center for Birds of Prey
Maitland

The Avian Reconditioning Center
Apopka

Natural Encounters, Inc.
Winter Haven

Georgia
Chattahoochee Nature Center
Roswell

Hawaii
Honolulu Zoo
Honolulu

Idaho
The Peregrine Fund
Boise

Illinois
Illinois Raptor Center
Decatur

Stillman Nature Center
South Barrington

Indiana
Indiana Raptor Center
Nashville

Iowa
Iowa Raptor Project
Solon

Kansas
Eagle Valley Raptor Center
Cheney

Kentucky
Raptor Rehabilitation of Kentucky, Inc.
Louisville

Louisiana
Audubon Zoo
New Orleans

Maine
Maine Wildlife Park
Gray

Maryland
Owl Moon Raptor Center
Boyds

Massachusetts
Blue Hills Trailside Museum
Milton

Drumlin Farm
Lincoln

EcoTarium
Worcester

Michigan
Leslie Science and Nature Center
Ann Arbor

Minnesota
Minnesota International Owl Center
Houston

The Raptor Center
St. Paul

Mississippi
Jackson Zoo
Jackson

Missouri
World Bird Sanctuary
Park

Montana
Montana Raptor Conservation Center
Bozeman

Owl Research Institute
Charlo

Nebraska
Fontenelle Forest
Bellevue

Nevada
Animal Ark Wildlife Sanctuary
Reno

New Hampshire
Squam Lakes Natural Science Center
Holderness

New Jersey
The Raptor Trust
Millington

New Mexico
Alameda Park Zoo
Alamogordo

Albuquerque Biological Park
Albuquerque

Living Desert Zoo and Gardens State Park
Sante Fe

New York
Braddock Bay Raptor Research
Honeoye Falls

Bronx Zoo
New York City

Buffalo Zoo
Buffalo

Hawk Creek Wildlife Center, Inc.
East Aurora

Wild Wings, Inc.
Honeoye Falls

North Carolina
Carolina Raptor Center
Huntersville

North Dakota
Dakota Zoo
Bismarck

Ohio
Glen Helen Ecology Institute
Yellow Springs

Oklahoma
Tulsa Zoo
Tulsa

Wild Care Foundation
Oklahoma City

Oregon
Cascades Raptor Center
Eugene

Pennsylvania
National Aviary
Pittsburgh

Rhode Island
Audubon Society of Rhode Island
Smithfield

South Carolina
The Center for Birds of Prey
Awendaw

South Dakota
Black Hills Raptor Center
Rapid City

Tennessee
American Eagle Foundation
Pigeon Forge

Texas
Blackland Prairie Raptor Center
Lucas

Fort Worth Zoo
Fort Worth

Houston Zoo
Houston

Utah
Tracy Aviary
Salt Lake City

Utah's Hogle Zoo
Salt Lake City

Vermont
Vermont Institute of Natural Science
Quechee

Virginia
The Raptor Conservancy of Virginia
Falls Church

The Wildlife Center of Virginia
Waynesboro

Washington
Point Defiance Zoo & Aquarium
Tacoma

Woodland Park Zoo
Seattle

West Virginia
Avian Conservation Center of Appalachia
Morgantown

Three Rivers Avian Center
Hinton

West Virginia Raptor Rehabilitation Center
Fairmont

Wisconsin
Hoo's Woods Raptor Center
Milton

Raptor Education Group, Inc.
Antigo

Wyoming
Teton Raptor Center
Wilson

CANADA

Alberta
Alberta Birds of Prey Foundation
Coaldale

Alberta Institute for Wildlife Conservation
Madden

Calgary Zoo
Calgary

British Columbia
OWL (Orphaned Wildlife) Rehabilitation Society
Delta

Pacific Northwest Raptors
Duncan

Sorco Raptor Rehab Centre
Oliver

Manitoba
Assiniboine Park Zoo
Winnipeg

Wildlife Haven Rehabilitation Center
Île des Chênes

New Brunswick
Magnetic Hill Zoo
Moncton

Newfoundland and Labrador
Salmonier Nature Park
Holyrood

Nova Scotia
Shubenacadie Wildlife Park
Shubenacadie

Two Rivers Wildlife Park
Huntington

Ontario
African Lion Safari
Hamilton

Bird Kingdom
Niagara Falls

Canadian Raptor Conservancy
Vittoria

Mountsberg Raptor Centre
Burlington

Toronto Zoo
Toronto

Saskatchewan
Saskatoon Zoo Society
Saskatoon

Quebec
UQROP (Quebec Union of Rehabilitators of Birds of Prey)
Saint-Hyacinthe

Zoo Ecomuseum
Montreal

INDEX

Northern Hawk Owl

Short-eared Owl

Metric Conversion Chart

WEIGHT		
To convert	to	multiply
ounces	grams	ounces by 28.35
pounds	grams	pounds by 453.5
pounds	kilograms	pounds by 0.45

LENGTH		
To convert	to	multiply
inches	millimeters	inches by 25.4
inches	centimeters	inches by 2.54